WITHDRAWN

Invented Truth

Soviet Reality and the
Literary Imagination of
Iurii Trifonov

Iurii Trifonov (*Courtesy of Ardis Photo Archives*)

Invented Truth

Soviet Reality and

the Literary Imagination

of Iurii Trifonov

Josephine Woll

Duke University Press Durham and London 1991

© 1991 Duke University Press
Printed in the United States of America
on acid-free paper ∞

Library of Congress Cataloging-in-Publication Data
Woll, Josephine.
    Invented truth : Soviet reality and the literary imagination of
Iurii Trifonov / Josephine Woll.
        p.   cm.
    Includes bibliographical references and index.
    ISBN 0-8223-1151-8
    1. Trifonov, I͡Urii Valentinovich, 1925–   —Criticism and
interpretation.   I. Title.
PG3489.R5Z77   1991
891.73'44—dc20   90-27834
                                                            CIP

Contents

Acknowledgments

M any people helped me during the years I worked on this book. Peter Kenez, Avi Soifer, Judith Woll, and Diana Woll Zurer were valued readers. Caryl Emerson's comments expanded my intellectual perspective as they deepened my understanding: they always do. Nancy Mitchell's good editorial judgment and literary sensitivity never flagged. I relied on the generosity of Soviet colleagues-turned-friends, especially Galina Belaia, Natalia Ivanova, Anatolii Bocharov, and Olga Miroshnichenko Trifonov.

Three organizations supported the work leading to this book, and I am indebted to them. In the spring of 1986 the Kennan Institute gave me my first uninterrupted opportunity to think about Trifonov. The National Council for Soviet and East European Research generously supported me during a sabbatical year. Thanks to the International Research and Exchanges Board I had an opportunity to live in Moscow and discuss ideas with Trifonov's readers, professional and otherwise. I spent several summers in Munich, using the library and picking the brains of the exceptionally knowledgeable and helpful staff at Radio Liberty/Radio Free Europe. Editors and tough, thoughtful readers at Duke University Press clarified the book's direction and enabled me to make it much better than what they first read. My thanks to Pam Morrison, Mindy Conner, and especially to Richard Rowson, who was interested at the beginning and was still interested at the end.

I am grateful for the sustaining moral support that came from many sources: from my husband, Abe Brumberg, who was charac-

teristically encouraging and uncharacteristically patient; from my
mother, Alice Woll; from colleagues at Howard University; from
family; and from several particular friends: Marcus Cunliffe, Phil
Gold, Darra Goldstein, Irving and Ilana Howe, Phyllis Palmer. This
book is dedicated to my aunt, Fanya Woll; I hope she would have
enjoyed reading it.

A Note on Transliteration

In bibliographical references and when Russian words are used in the text, the Library of Congress system of transliteration (without diacritical marks) is used. For Russian names in the English text a simplified, commonsense version of this is used.

Introduction

Soviet readers have known Iurii Trifonov's books since his first novel was published forty years ago. They eagerly bought out the large print runs in which his books were normally published. Especially after 1968, when many of the best Russian writers were no longer able to publish inside the Soviet Union, they regarded Trifonov as one of the few good and honest writers left to them. In the last five years Trifonov has regularly been cited as a precursor of *glasnost'*, a writer who examined Soviet history long before such examination became permissible, if not indeed obligatory. Most of the other writers of the late 1960s and 1970s whom readers admired and considered morally trustworthy, such as Valentin Rasputin, Viktor Astafev, Vasilii Shukshin, and Fedor Abramov, spoke for, and to, readers one generation removed from their peasant roots in the Russian countryside. Iurii Trifonov spoke for, and to, the urban Soviet intelligentsia.

In the West, Trifonov is less widely known than other Soviet writers such as Isaac Babel, Boris Pasternak, Mikhail Bulgakov, and Aleksandr Solzhenitsyn. Yet these authors, whose books have become part of the intellectual culture of liberally educated men and women wherever they reside, were not really Soviet writers at all. Though they lived and wrote in the Soviet Union, they were by and large unable to publish within the Soviet system. Often they came to Western readers' attention because of their "outlaw" status, although they remain part of Western consciousness because of their quality. A book written for the drawer, like *The Master and*

Margarita, does not attempt to compromise with the system because it never intends to be part of it. Even works by Solzhenitsyn, who did hope for their publication within the Soviet Union, show much less willingness to adapt to the system.

The works of authors who were excluded—or chose to exclude themselves—from the system reveal little about the system beyond its contemptible stupidity. Such writers contribute little to our understanding of the interlocking of culture and politics that has been the context for officially published literature. The fiction of entirely orthodox writers is equally unhelpful, although in a different way. Although it can be a rich source of information about accepted and acceptable values and attitudes, such literature is "didactic and unimaginative, the perishable output of safe writers."[1] As such, almost by definition it does not seek to trespass beyond officially imposed limits. Authors of orthodox literature do not need to use their artistic skill to convey more—or other—than what their limited freedom grants them.

Not many writers in recent Soviet history fall between these two extremes. Iurii Trifonov does. Like the work of a few other writers of integrity who continued to publish through official Soviet channels, Trifonov's fiction offers the best opportunity to understand the intersection of politics and art as it existed in the late 1960s and 1970s.

Within that intersection between politics and literature, especially as the relationship developed in the Soviet Union after Khrushchev's fall and before Gorbachev's rise to power, an emphasis on the political component generates one kind of question, while an emphasis on the literary component generates another. Trifonov's fiction, particularly in the 1970s, examined essentially taboo subjects: the intellectual and moral rot of the Stalinist era, and the violence done to morality in the Bolshevik era that was perpetrated by the Bolsheviks and clearly linked with its Stalinist spawn. The cultural climate when Trifonov published those works was repressive. Censorship, though unpredictable, was severe and institutionalized. How, then, was Trifonov able to publish works which defied or circumvented the prohibitions that stifled other authors? What circumstances made it possible? Were the reasons primarily literary or primarily political?

Reverse the emphasis, and the acknowledged indivisibility of politics and culture in the Soviet context focuses on the literary component of that unity. What is the literary effect and what are the aesthetic consequences of censorship on the work of a gifted writer? One must assume that Trifonov, like every other Soviet writer who wrote for publication (rather than for the drawer), internalized censorship constraints. Nevertheless, he managed to say a great deal that seemed to be prohibited. How did Trifonov adapt his style, his language, and his narrative strategies to counteract the exigencies of publishing reality? And how did he perceive the role of the artist within Soviet society—the artist's responsibilities and the artist's opportunities?

In the Soviet Union today, an infinitely more tolerant publishing climate permits nearly anything at all to be said, and printed, without fear. Yet amid the spate of newly discovered classics, the recovered émigré legacy, and the works of younger writers now entering the literary marketplace, Trifonov's fiction endures. It is worth trying to understand why.

Since the inception of the Soviet Union—indeed, even during the centuries of tsarist rule in Russia—the state has consistently determined what is acceptable in the arts, and especially in literature. The criteria have varied, as has the rigor with which they have been applied, but they have always been primarily political.[2] Soviet censorship has differed from tsarist censorship in two salient literary respects, apart from the variation in types of sanctions levied on the offending writer. The first distinction is between proscription and prescription; the second, between product and process. Keeping in mind that the kind and degree of tsarist censorship depended on the particular tsar, and that Soviet censorship under Stalin was far different from what it has been since Stalin's death, Nabokov's generalization is nonetheless valid:

> Nineteenth-century Russia was oddly enough a free country: books and writers might be banned and banished, censors might be rogues and fools, be-whiskered Tsars might stamp and storm; but that wonderful discovery of Soviet times, the method of making the entire literary corporation write what the state deems fit—this method was unknown in old Russia.... In Russia before the Soviet rule there did exist restrictions, but no orders were given to artists.[3]

By "orders" Nabokov had in mind, of course, socialist realism, a doctrine which by the 1960s had already lost much of its force, if less of its rhetorical domination of literature.[4]

With Stalin's death and the ensuing alleviation of fear, writers were again subject far more to proscription than to prescription, a comparatively light burden. But Stalin's reign had also created a system of institutions and a bureaucracy designed to control the creative process, and after his death that system remained substantially intact. In general, pre-Soviet censorship, especially severe under Nicholas I, targeted the product. In literature, that meant the manuscript: Pushkin's supposedly blasphemous "Gavriliada," Lermontov's angry poetic denunciation of court responsibility for Pushkin's death, Gogol's Captain Kopeikin in *Dead Souls*. The process of creating that product, from inspiration to execution, was left up to the individual artist. There were no institutional structures that governed or even organized the creation of literature like those that came into existence in the Soviet era, particularly after 1934.[5]

Those structures systematized control of the creative process as a means to controlling the product that reached the reader. They proved more durable than the dogma of socialist realism, which was nearly moribund by the late 1960s and 1970s. The system of censorship, in contrast, functioned quite well. Its exponents were literary functionaries in the Writers' Union, journal editors, and official employees of the Censorship Board (*Glavlit*). The power of the Writers' Union grew in inverse proportion to the roles of socialist realism and the Glavlit. The former was "declared to be a flexible method for writers, not a dogmatic, exclusive style," and the latter became "a backstop to prevent the revelation of state secrets, or the mention of peoples, places, and events considered taboo."[6]

The Brezhnev era, dubbed under Gorbachev "the period of stagnation," was indeed a stifling period, particularly for the intellectual and cultural pluralism that had begun to emerge under Khrushchev. If Khrushchev's fall from power was the political marker of the end of the old, the cultural marker of the new period was the Siniavskii-Daniel trial in February 1966. If Brezhnev's death marked the end, more or less, of *zastoi* (stagnation), its last cultural gasp was the *Metropol* affair of 1979; and Gorbachev's 1986 telephone call to Sakharov in Gorki was one of the first and most striking symbols of *glasnost'*. The years between were punctuated by a series of domestic and international events that reinforced the atmosphere of repression.

Initiative and imagination, whether in pursuit of new economic strategies or greater artistic freedom, were banked, if not smothered. Beginning in 1966, in Ronald Hingley's words, "the literary censorship was unobtrusively strengthened and rendered more sophisticated, being applied with special rigor to works and periodicals enjoying a large circulation."[7] The letter Aleksandr Solzhenitsyn sent to the Writers' Union when he was refused the right to speak at the Fourth Congress, in May 1967, addressed the literary aspect:

Under the obfuscating label of Glavlit, this censorship—which is not provided for in the Constitution and is therefore illegal, and which is nowhere publicly labeled as such—imposes a yoke on our literature and gives people unversed in literature arbitrary control over writers. . . . Many members of the [Writers'] Union and even many of the delegates at this Congress, know how they themselves have bowed to the pressures of the censorship and made concessions in the structure and concept of their books—changing chapters, pages, paragraphs, or sentences, giving them innocuous titles—just for the sake of seeing them finally in print, even if it meant distorting them irremediably. . . . Literature cannot develop in between the categories of "permitted" and "not permitted," "about this you may write" and "about this you may not."[8]

Needless to say, Solzhenitsyn's letter did not appear in *Literaturnaia gazeta*, to which it had been sent, or in any other Soviet publication, though the Western press immediately published it. (Soviet publication occurred only in 1989.) The Writers' Union, far from heeding Solzhenitsyn's words, used the 1967 Congress as an occasion to tighten its hold on literature; in the following years its control of the major literary journals increased, and its links with the Communist party were strengthened. The two bodies became roughly parallel in structure and procedure; union plenums were coordinated with party congresses in order to increase ideological decorum.[9] The party appointed orthodox bureaucrats, often writers in name only, to positions of power; so-called released secretaries, full-time bureaucrats "released" from other duties—such as writing—ran the "business" of literature. They were, indeed, "substantially or principally engaged in manipulating, supervising and determining the activities, privileges and emoluments of subordinate scribes."[10]

The Writers' Union was abetted—indeed, empowered—in its control by the immense range of its activities. It operated printing presses, ran a major publishing house (Sovetskii pisatel'), and over-saw all major literary journals and periodicals, which regularly underwent official review by the union Secretariat. But its power was by no means restricted to the purely literary arena. The union determined the amount of writers' pensions and disability income, their access to housing and relatively luxurious "rest homes," lec-ture tours, travel funds (especially the nearly unobtainable hard cur-rency), and a host of other perquisites and privileges.[11] When the Writers' Union took the step of expelling a member—Boris Paster-nak in October 1958, Aleksandr Solzhenitsyn in November 1969, Vladimir Voinovich in 1974—it imposed a serious financial burden on that individual, apart from the opprobrium of his colleagues. (Only 7 of the 6,790 members of the union protested the expulsion of Solzhenitsyn; one of them was Trifonov.) Twenty years after the Solzhenitsyn affair, the Writers' Union still controlled all these ac-tivities and sanctions, affecting the lives and livelihoods of writers far beyond the single issue of publication.

A complementary bureaucracy controlling publication—specif-ically, ensuring the correct ideological content of all printed mat-ter—is the State Committee for the Press, created in 1963. Under Brezhnev this organization expanded its reach. Two plans had to be fulfilled: one economic (a production plan), the other ideological (a "thematic" plan). The former plan stressed production, the tra-ditional Soviet orientation for all industries; the latter evaluated *ideinost'* and *partiinost'* (conformity with the party line), whatever it happened to be.

Apart from individual obscenities like the Solzhenitsyn case, the whole system *as a system* encouraged both conformity and a kind of hypertrophy. The publishing industry, like all other Soviet indus-tries, fulfilled its plan by producing a certain number of books, not by satisfying readers. Managers were judged by production, not sales, figures. The easiest, and surely ideologically safest, course was to publish massive editions of such books as Brezhnev's collected speeches. Moreover, Soviet authors had and still have a vested in-terest in the system, since their royalties are based on the number of copies of their books that are printed—a figure determined by the State Committee on the Press—and not on the number of copies sold. Members of the union Secretariat have routinely had their books published in print runs of staggering size.[12]

In the period when Trifonov was publishing his most important work, a manuscript submitted for publication in a literary journal was routinely vetted by a series of officials or offices, in the following sequence:

1. The editor of the appropriate department of the journal (e.g., prose or poetry)
2. The head of the journal's editorial department
3. The journal's "responsible" editor (*otvetstvennyi redaktor*)
4. The journal's deputy chief editor
5. The journal's chief editor
6. The censor (representative of Glavlit), who could work only on manuscripts sent on by journals and publishing houses
7. The district or regional party committee
8. The Russian republic branch of Goskomizdat (the state committee)
9. The all-union Goskomizdat.[13]

The importance of editors in the censorship process, obvious from this list, has been confirmed by virtually every émigré writer who worked within the system in the 1960s and 1970s.[14] Their importance is magnified by the enormous readerships of the major literary journals; the monthly magazines *Novyi mir* and *Oktiabr'*, for instance, had circulations of half a million, and copies were passed from reader to reader, thus reaching many more than the circulation figure suggests. A novel printed in one of these journals, then, typically reached many times the number of readers than the same text in its eventually published book form.

Because they were held responsible for ideological lapses, editors were often more cautious than the Glavlit censors. Anatolii Gladilin, a popular writer who left the Soviet Union in the mid-1970s, satirized this odd relationship:

> In principle, every worker on the editorial staff was supposed to protect the interests of the magazine. But here's the typical picture. An issue has just been cleared by the censorship office. The chief secretary picks up the telephone and calls the censor himself: "Did you read it carefully? Didn't you find anything? Well, page seventeen, fifth line from the top, doesn't that passage bother you? No? It's permissible? And then—page fifty-five, eighth line from the bottom, doesn't that call up some associations? And the next paragraph down, I think that sounds kind of strange . . ."[15]

Since party ideology shifted, at times unpredictably, editors were understandably nervous. Their own decisions were subject to review on a higher level, especially if the manuscript raised—or might be construed possibly to raise—issues of any sensitivity.

There were a few editors who earned reputations for their courage and intellectual integrity. Foremost among them was Aleksandr Tvardovskii, editor of *Novyi mir* throughout the 1960s. Tvardovskii's fame, especially in the West, rests primarily on his advocacy of Solzhenitsyn, both when he cagily inveigled Khrushchev's personal approval for publishing *One Day in the Life of Ivan Denisovich* and in his later efforts to publish *Cancer Ward*. But Tvardovskii consistently attempted to bring out interesting, honest work in *Novyi mir*, and he used his considerable knowledge and skills to exploit temporary abatements of the repression. He was one of the few editors to do so; patently, the system discouraged both writers and editors from taking risks, encouraging instead mediocrity and caution. Within a year of Solzhenitsyn's expulsion from the Writers' Union, Tvardovskii was stripped of the editorship of *Novyi mir*; he died soon after. The journal, as edited by his successor, Kosolapov, overflowed with pedestrian fiction by authors whose names are hardly mentioned now (for example, Roman Solntsev, Valerii Povoliaev, Anatolii Krivonosov, Aleksandr Kharchikov, Iurii Antropov, and Iosif Gerasimov), and with a profusion of translations.

Despite the intensified censorship of the late 1960s and 1970s, and the extraliterary sanctions imposed on writers who transgressed the boundaries of the permissible, evasions of the official publishing system did occur. A few controversial texts barred from the main periodicals appeared in provincial journals: the Strugatskii brothers' antiutopian "science fiction" novel *Snail on the Slope*, for instance, came out in the journal *Baikal*—or at least its odd-numbered chapters did, while the even-numbered chapters appeared two years later in Leningrad. Thanks to authorial or editorial sleight of hand, a few "illicit" texts were incorporated into otherwise unexceptionable ones,[16] but such instances of specific legerdemain were few.

During the decade and a half after Khrushchev's fall, members of the creative intelligentsia experienced a continuous erosion of their freedom. Writers were barred from official publication channels because the contents and/or style of their work violated official canons. Some lost access because of their extraliterary activities— signing petitions on behalf of Sakharov or Marchenko, giving shelter to Solzhenitsyn—and many transgressed in both word and deed. Their response was to develop alternative channels, particularly the astonishing phenomenon of *samizdat*, literature that circulated unofficially in typescript and manuscript.

The bulk of *samizdat* consisted of documents, trial transcripts, protest letters, and appeals. But a number of major literary texts circulated as well: Evgeniia Ginzburg's memoirs, Nadezhda Mandelstam's memoirs, Vasilii Grossman's novels *Life and Fate* and *Forever Flowing*, Anna Akhmatova's poem "Requiem," all of Solzhenitsyn's unpublished work, Vladimov's *Faithful Ruslan*, Voinovich's *Life and Extraordinary Adventures of Private Ivan Chonkin*, and so on. Many *samizdat* texts found their way abroad and were published in Russian by Western émigré presses and in translations.[17] Some work bypassed *samizdat* channels and went directly to Western journals and publishing houses.

If writers chose to circulate their manuscripts via the *samizdat* network, they reached an extremely small readership; if they sent their manuscripts out of the country, for *tamizdat* publication, they reached more readers but not their primary audience of fellow countrymen. A number of writers, as well as other prominent members of the cultural elite, chose or were forced to emigrate in the 1970s. Jews, for whom emigration was easier than for any other single group, comprised a large proportion of that cultural exile. Russian literature became a multicentered enterprise: its headquarters may still have been Moscow's Central House of Literature, but branches functioned in Paris, Munich, New York, Tel Aviv, London, and Cavendish, Vermont.

Yet even during the worst years of the Brezhnev era, art that defied the system and circumvented its apparently inflexible strictures was produced within the Soviet Union. Before he went abroad in 1983, for example, theater director Iurii Liubimov spent twenty years fighting for permission to stage controversial productions at the Taganka Theater; although permission was sometimes rescinded at the last minute, he occasionally got what he wanted. The body of fiction that arose in the early 1950s and was given the rubric "village prose" treated with integrity such sensitive subjects as the abandonment of traditional values and the damage wrought on the countryside by technological "progress." If some of these works were nostalgic evocations of Russian rural traditions, with only muted political implications, others conveyed "outspoken criticism of Party policy as imposed on the villages."[18] The village prose movement (those conventionally associated with it often reject that label) was not a consistent darling of the literary establishment, but it gained respectability in the 1970s. One of its leading writers, Fedor Abramov, won the State Prize for Literature in 1975.[19]

Sometimes such works served as a kind of lightning rod for the regime: while they were critical of certain aspects of Soviet society, their criticism was far less sweeping (and therefore less dangerous) than the writing of, for instance, Solzhenitsyn and Voinovich. Moreover, while the Soviet state was prepared to expel beyond its borders irredeemable individuals, it did so reluctantly. The government was not happy that so many members of the creative intelligentsia were leaving for the West. Its most powerful inducement to writers was the promise—part of a mutually advantageous, if tacit, contract—that their work could be published. Andrei Siniavskii, who has lived in the West since 1973, described the impact of the emigration, and dissent generally, on state control:

> With the appearance of ventures which the state interprets as hostile to itself—*samizdat*, the activities of the dissidents and so on—the censorship has tended to be more lenient with certain official writers, who are therefore permitted to deal quite boldly with subjects which, although not the most burning in social and political terms, are nonetheless of considerable peripheral interest, like the subject of the Soviet past and individual destinies. You thus have writers operating completely within the official limits who nevertheless write interesting works. And the state is obliged to tolerate them, because if they banned them completely they would all go straight into *samizdat* or emigrate to the West. . . . The decision of so many writers to become dissidents is forcing the authorities to somewhat loosen the screws.[20]

The terms were rarely, if ever, spelled out, and they could be changed without warning. Yet those who, whatever their privately held and privately articulated views, avoided public expressions of protest won from the state a little room to maneuver. Writers were sometimes rewarded for rejecting the option of *tamizdat*, or publication abroad. Anatolii Rybakov, for instance, turned down many offers to publish *Children of the Arbat* in the West. Although his loyalty did not enable him to publish *that* novel in the Soviet Union until the onset of *glasnost'*, it may well have helped him in 1978 when he published *Heavy Sand*, a novel that contained a controversial depiction of Belorussian complicity with the Nazis in the destruction of the local Jewish ghetto. Such elbowroom was small, but it could be meaningfully exploited, and it often was.

Explicit systemic criticism of contemporary Soviet society was not tolerated in the Brezhnev years; neither was explicit examination of the Stalin era and its consequences in modern Soviet society. The relationship between Leninism and Stalinism was certainly taboo. Nevertheless, such issues could be alluded to, and attentive readers (or viewers) were relied upon to draw certain inferences. Writers who chose to write for publication within the system embedded their ideas in an Aesopian art that absolutely required and assumed alert "respondents." Writers who wrote solely for *samizdat* and *tamizdat* could eschew Aesopian language, but much that ended up in *samizdat* was either written in a period of relaxation that then vanished or in the hopes of future relaxation—that is, with the possibility of official publication in mind, hence with some degree of coding.

Aesopian "language" need not be verbal. In Liubimov's stage productions of classic—even canonic—plays at the Taganka, allusions were often coded in sets or in acting but appeared nowhere on paper for the censors to see in advance. Indeed, last-minute cancellations of Liubimov's productions sometimes resulted from censors' attendance at dress rehearsals, where innocent lines suddenly sounded suspect when acted out.[21] When the Leningrad director Georgii Tovstonogov produced Griboedov's classic comedy *Woe from Wit*, the audience applauded even before the actors appeared, because they saw flashed onto the curtain Pushkin's lament for having been born in Russia "with feeling and talent." (Within a few days of the opening the "epigraph" was banned.)[22]

For writers, reader complicity is essential. As Lev Loseff's study of Aesopian language shows, a variety of "screens" divert the censor, while a variety of "markers" direct the reader. Mikhail Shatrov's play *The Bolsheviks*, which depicts the Bolshevik leadership's debate on the use of mass terror against the opposition in 1918, relied on its audience's historical hindsight: "the audience knows that the terror which the characters describe as a supremely temporary measure, for which they seek convincing humane arguments, will drag on for decades, be unleashed upon all who would promote human values and bring on, incidentally, the political or the physical demise of the very persons who appear on stage."[23]

It seems paradoxical. Why don't the same markers that alert the reader to the coded message alert the editor or censor? If screens obscure the censor's vision, why don't they also obscure the reader's? Often they do. Many readers take texts at face value and ignore subtexts, while censors can be sensitive readers. But successful Aesopian art depends on "the joint possession by author and reader (sender and receiver) of one and the same piece of information."[24] More, it depends on their sharing the same point of view and the same general values. Without that shared knowledge and stance, the apprehension of text misses a dimension. Even knowledgeable and sophisticated Westerners, for instance, need to have song texts (by, say, Okudzhava or Vysotskii) deciphered for them by Soviet friends, or they sit bewildered in a Soviet theater amid appreciative laughter or applause. Without that shared point of view, Shatrov's depiction of the Bolshevik debate, with its final justification of terror, merely corroborates officially sanctified values. An inquisitive reader might read a diatribe against existentialism in order to ferret out the main ideas of existentialism, while a censor or a less curious or more conventional reader might simply regard that same volume as a defense of dialectical materialism.

Iurii Trifonov stayed in-system in the 1970s. Like any other writer functioning within the system, his success in reaching the reader was only partly under his control: much of it depended on macropolitical factors not connected with him, or literary politics on which his influence was minimal. He was, however, in control of one set of means to reach the reader he had in mind—namely, the literary means of tropes, metaphors, language, and narrative structures. The fiction he wrote between 1968 and his death in 1981 examined painful themes in Soviet life: degraded values, betrayal, fatherlessness, the falsification of the past, and the bankruptcy of the present. His work met the response it did because in some sense he spoke for, and to, millions of his countrymen.

Two simultaneous, contrasting developments contributed to Trifonov's post-1968 prominence. As more Soviet writers moved underground or abroad, the literary environs in which Trifonov's work appeared became increasingly drab. At the same time he himself became increasingly bold, in both the range and the depth of his work. *House on the Embankment* and *The Old Man* would have startled readers whenever they might have been published. Given the grayness (as *glasnost'*-era Soviet criticism repeatedly describes the literature of that period) and mediocrity of most contemporary, officially published Soviet prose, Trifonov's works assumed an extraordinary importance.

Although authors who remained in the Soviet Union and published their work in officially sponsored literary outlets were by and large undistinguished, they were not necessarily working within socialist realist parameters. As early as the 1950s one explicit reaction against socialist realist norms involved a much greater emphasis on individual, private experience within the societal context.[25] Another, rejecting the implacably forward-looking stance of socialist realist art, turned backward, to pre-Petrine Russia and traditional Russian folk art.[26] The best of the village prose writers depicted a world of values and morality lost and often destroyed by human forces; implicitly, they rejected modern Soviet society.[27] They manipulated the conventions of socialist realism to produce highly suggestive but ultimately elusive meanings.[28]

In this literary atmosphere Trifonov was unusual for two reasons. First, he fixed a clear—at times mercilessly clear—light on the contemporary urban intelligentsia, particularly its cynicism and consumerism, and on the degraded state of that handful of ideals in which scions of the intelligentsia still believed but were unable to act on. As the Soviet critic Igor Zolotusskii recently wrote, "Trifonov was the first to begin writing about the ''60s' men. He spoke about them in *The Exchange*, in *Long Goodbye* and in *Another Life*. Other members of that generation wrote about them as well, and wrote impartially, but those books (Aksenov's *Burn*, Maksimov's *Seven Days of Creation*) left for the West, together with their authors."[29]

Moreover, Trifonov's fictional examinations of the Soviet past, especially in *House on the Embankment* and *The Old Man*, startled readers accustomed to a deafening silence on the Stalin "excesses" and a ritualized literary glorification of the formation and early years of the Soviet state. A comment on Trifonov's hero Sergei Troitskii (from *Another Life*) applies equally to Trifonov himself: "In conditions of *neglasnost'*, that is to say officially supported dishonesty, the secret and half-forbidden tempts. Thus the recent disciple of Clio [the muse of history] almost begins to serve Hecate [goddess of ghosts, conjurer of dreams and spirits of the dead]."[30] Other artistic visions—or versions—of the past were available in novels like *Doctor Zhivago*, Grossman's *Forever Flowing* and Chukovskaia's *Sofia Petrovna*, and in scholarship like Aleksandr Nekrich's *June 22, 1941* and the Medvedev brothers' works. But such books, like Aksenov's and Maksimov's, were accessible only in *samizdat*; that is, they were inaccessible to the overwhelming majority of Soviet readers. Readers were amazed that Trifonov's books were published, and they were exhilarated by what they read. The landscape of largely banal and predictable fiction against which the books appeared merely enhanced their impact.

Even in the Brezhnev years Trifonov was not unique in finding a way to examine the moral imperatives created by Soviet history and the ethical dilemmas of Soviet society. But his ability to suggest what he could not say out loud was unusual. Lev Kopelev, a dissident who was himself ultimately forced to leave the Soviet Union, said about Trifonov in 1977, "He gets everything in. He only doesn't mention things that are specifically forbidden. He assumes the reader already knows what he is alluding to."[31]

Trifonov did more than allude to taboo subjects and shrouded events or periods of Soviet history. He linked the moral expediency of the nation's past—whether in the service of idealistic ends or as a means of self-aggrandizement—with the spiritual degeneration of subsequent generations. In the words of Victor Toporov, "Trifonov and his heroes . . . knew what they had been intended to be—and what they had not become—and they knew, though they didn't say so out loud, why that had happened."[32] Other good writers—Shukshin and Rasputin, for instance—wrote about the victims of the transformation of Soviet society, people who had little understanding of and less control over their own lives. Trifonov took his readers inside the transformation process itself. He rendered it from the point of view of those members of the urban intelligentsia who had "made" the Soviet Union and must live with the results, the point of view of those who abetted Stalinism and must now live with themselves. Many artists dealt with the national trauma of fatherlessness, of orphaned children and destroyed families. Trifonov, in re-creating the anguish of the abandoned child, linked that abandonment with a moral climate generated by specific historical events known to every one of his readers.

Since the end of 1986, the Soviet cultural scene has changed radically. Indeed, one of the first signals of *glasnost'* was the publication of Trifonov's unfinished novella *The Disappearance*, with its unusually direct depiction of an NKVD search and the fear-sodden atmosphere of 1937–38. Another was the Taganka Theater's performance of *House on the Embankment*, a production that had been banned after its creator, Iurii Liubimov, left the Soviet Union until Gorbachev himself, backstage one evening in the fall of 1986, asked the Taganka's director why the Trifonov work was no longer performed.

The changes have affected both the nature of cultural artifacts produced and the means by which they are created and distributed. Thus, for instance, film studios and many theaters now operate with near-total autonomy in both aesthetic and financial spheres. Prior censorship has virtually disappeared. The rehabilitation of writers as different as Gumilev, Nabokov, and Solzhenitsyn, and of erstwhile political "demons" like Bukharin and Trotskii, has become commonplace. (According to Aleksandr Iakovlev, some two million victims of the purges were rehabilitated by the Politburo Commission on Rehabilitation between its establishment in September 1987 and June 1990.)

This extraordinary process, an evolving and dynamic recovery of the nation's political and cultural history, has destroyed the constraints of more than half a century. Issues that Trifonov, in his time, treated "courageously but mutely" (in Toporov's phrase) are now regularly debated in public forums and in the media. Yet despite the far greater candor in recently published works, Trifonov's fiction continues to be read and discussed. He is repeatedly cited by liberal critics—Ivanova, Zolotusskii, Dedkov, Anninskii, Belaia—as a precursor of *glasnost'*. He is a silent partner in a dialogue initiated by many younger writers, some of whom are friendly, respectful, and even admiring (Boris Ekimov, Evgenii Popov, and Tatiana Tolstaia, for example), while others are more ironic and distanced (Vladimir Makanin). Either way, by virtue of his own work as well as by the press of circumstances, Trifonov is one of their chief collocutors, one of the few whose work was readily available for emulation and argument at a time when their literary consciousness was developing.

For Soviet writers, and for Soviet readers generally, Trifonov's books remain a source of both aesthetic pleasure and moral weight. Undoubtedly he made compromises in order to continue publishing within the Soviet Union. Yet he was more than a purveyor of "sanctioned" truth or half-truth. He developed a style that was sufficiently elliptical at once to reveal and conceal his own views. It closely corresponded to his own sense of the complex relationships of the individual and history, of time past and time present, of experience and the artistic representation of experience. What he managed to say, and how he managed to say it, is what this book is fundamentally about.

I

Preparations

Trifonov stood out among his fellow writers for several reasons. He succeeded in publishing works that defied or circumvented stifling prohibitions; he developed or adapted to publishing exigencies a literary style that at once conveyed and concealed his thoughts; and he managed to do so without sacrificing artistic quality. But he did those things in the second half of a thirty-year career, most notably in the last decade of his writing. The fiction he wrote between 1950 and 1966 generally conformed to the prevailing literary dogma of the period. It was competent, and readers liked it, but it was artistically undistinguished and offered little challenge to the cultural status quo.

Trifonov's earlier work is revealing, however, in one respect: themes and techniques developed to much greater effect in his mature work are also present in relatively primitive versions. Hence this chapter describes, without detailed analysis, how Trifonov conceived and introduced those recurrent themes in his earlier works as well as in the fully mature novellas that comprise the "Moscow trilogy" (published between 1969 and 1971), *Impatience* (1973), and *Another Life* (1975).

Iurii Trifonov's literary career began in 1950 when his novel *Students (Studenty)*, written in 1948 and 1949, was published in the leading literary journal of the time, *Novyi mir*.[1] He received his professional training at the Gorky Literary Institute, the most prestigious literary hothouse in the Soviet Union, from a faculty that

17

included such notables as novelists Konstantin Paustovskii and Konstantin Fedin. Indeed, Trifonov's first novel is about the Gorky Literary Institute, fictionalized as Moscow's Pedagogical Institute. In *Students*, as in nearly all his work, Trifonov drew his subject matter from his own experiences and those of his family. *Students* portrays a group of students in the postwar years who work, study, love, and quarrel against the background of the last years of Stalin's reign.

Students was an immediate success with readers and was awarded a Stalin Prize, third degree. Recalling his early success from a distance of twenty years, Trifonov attributed the popularity of *Students* to its realistic depiction of Moscow student life. Most of the best books published in those years were about the war, but readers wanted books about their own familiar, contemporary life. "In the history of Russia," Trifonov wrote, "there was never a more grateful readership than after the end of the war. . . . [*Students* contained] a certain everyday truth, details reminiscent of life."[2] Vera Dunham suggests that *Students* satisfied a deeper hunger, however, than the need to escape from the oversized heroism and all-too-familiar tragedy portrayed in war fiction. Squashed into communal apartments and overcrowded trams, readers longed for at least the prospect of bourgeois comforts and beauty. Trifonov portrayed the lives of the affluent and privileged—replete with pink lampshades, kitch knick-knacks, and mauve wallpaper—neutrally, without criticism, and thereby legitimated that longing. He offered "the hope that the entire middle class might some day share the life-style of the few."[3]

Attention to the details and texture of everyday middle-class life later became a trademark of Trifonov's prose. In *Students* it added freshness to what was in many ways a conventional novel of its period. The late 1940s and early 1950s, the last gasp of Stalinism, have been called "the bleakest and most sterile [years] in Soviet literature."[4] Most Soviet prose written during these years was sheathed in the straitjacket of socialist realism. Ideological purity, populism, and obedience to the party line were still demanded; the "positive hero" still triumphed, though his profile had changed somewhat from its earlier versions.[5]

The positive hero of *Students* is the deliberately deheroized young war veteran, Vadim Belov. Slow but steady, he is contrasted with his girlfriend Lena and his friend Sergei, both fellow students at the institute and both far more brilliant and attractive to others than

Belov. Despite their éclat, they are ultimately inferior to Belov; indeed, their very brilliance is suspect. "As soon as serious effort, and intense and consistent . . . work are called for, both Lena and Sergei set themselves up in opposition to the collective, stand apart from it."⁶ Belov is diligent, industrious, reliable, and, despite a tincture of envy, a decent man. His positive qualities thus more than compensate for the mediocrity of his talents.

Students has an ideological focus that also conforms to the norms of the period. The anticosmopolitan campaign of the late 1940s, directed primarily at intellectuals, is reflected in the campaign against a professor of literature in the institute, Kozelskii. Kozelskii was one of a number of fictional professors in that period, for, as Dunham observes, "in the terrible last years of Stalin's life, entirely nonfictional intellectuals swelled the ranks of those behind barbed wires. And fiction, no matter how false, optimistic and obfuscating, kept pointing by reflex to the victims."⁷ Kozelskii is eventually dismissed for "formalism" and "toadyism," charges common enough during that period. These are not presented as rational indictments in the novel; rather, they are acknowledged as invective. Nevertheless, Trifonov adjudges Kozelskii guilty—or rather, he allows Kozelskii's childhood friend, now dean of the institute, to pass judgment: "I will say no more about your formalism or your estheticism. These are only the results. The causes are more complicated. . . . The causes lie in the fact that all these forty years, these stormy, difficult forty years which have roused the whole world, you have not lived correctly. You were concerned with one thing only: how best to protect yourself against being bruised! You chose a style for yourself, that of comfortable skepticism."⁸

Students was an extremely popular book, but its ideological conformism was hard for Trifonov to live with in later years. He recognized that a writer could not repudiate his own work; all he could do was distance himself from Students and its simplistic and categorical judgments. In his 1976 novella The House on the Embankment, he assayed a kind of literary expiation, reworking the basic elements of Students in the light of his mature understanding. As the critic Evgenii Shklovskii perceptively comments, Students is the book that gave Trifonov his horror of clichés and cliché-ridden thoughts. After Students, and as a result of it, he avoided taking upon himself the role of judge and moralist.⁹

Students is an immature work, and artistically awkward. Yet many of its themes and characteristics recur in Trifonov's later work. It therefore offers a starting point from which to trace Trifonov's development. Thus, for example, the language, details, and mores of everyday life—what in Russian is termed *byt*—are rendered with a keen sense of the rhythm and color of quotidian reality, though they lack psychological depth. After years of blacked-out war bleakness, the Moscow of *Students* is being filled with new buildings bedizened with waxed floors and enameled elevators (to use Dunham's examples). The city is not merely the physical setting for the action of the novel; it almost takes part in the action; it seems to resemble a human character.

Two of the central preoccupations of Trifonov's work are already present in *Students*. One, virtually fully formed, is the depiction of childhood as an evanescent idyll. Its perfection stems in part from ignorance of what will inevitably destroy it. As early as *Students*, written when Trifonov was in his early twenties, this image of childhood is ripe. Trifonov presents it here with the same evocative mixture of wonder and pain that is evident in his very last stories thirty years later. His sense of the childhood idyll and its imminent destruction did not change emotionally, nor did it develop intellectually. Its immutability is rooted in emotional trauma; in his later work Trifonov merely added information.

Trifonov's second major concern is the interdependence of men and the times in which they live. Unlike the first, this is an issue to be apprehended intellectually as well as emotionally, and Trifonov grappled with it throughout his creative life. As his understanding of its complexity changed and deepened over the years, so did his fictional presentation. From the superficial and inchoate relationship between individuals' ethics and behavior and their era portrayed in *Students*, Trifonov moved to a subtle and tragic concept of the individual's inescapable responsibility for his time and its sometimes unforeseeable consequences. In the work of his last decade, however he varied the context, character, and point of view, this theme predominates.

The sixteen years that separated the publication of *Students* from Trifonov's next major work, *The Campfire's Glow* (*Otblesk kostra*), produced a play, a number of stories, and sports and travel sketches. Although these were not entirely barren years, they were frustrating, uncreative years in which Trifonov sought the voice and genre that would liberate him to write what and as he wished. Flashes of what we now know to be characteristic techniques appear: in the very early story "White Gates," for instance, the onset of the war is rendered retrospectively, through a prism of homecomings and reminiscences. (The story, though published in the 1959 collection *Under the Sun* [*Pod solntsem*], was dated 1947–52.) The childhood motif appears in what later became a familiar dual perspective: "The joyful, natural life of children in a nearly paradisical garden, who don't know about future woes and misfortunes, [is contrasted with] the knowledge we share with the author that this joy is already threatened by war, by historical cataclysm."[10]

Because of the educational and ideological burden literature has traditionally borne in the Soviet Union, Soviet writers were regularly sent on trips around the country to broaden their experience. Such trips were meant to expose them to "real" workers, for instance, whether on construction sites or collective farms, or to offer opportunities to gain firsthand knowledge of genuine popular culture, via folk music or folklore; the folklore expeditions were especially common in the 1930s. In line with this tradition, Trifonov was sent by *Novyi mir* to the Turkmen Republic to observe the construction of the Kara-Kum Canal. The eventual result was his 1963 novel *Slaking the Thirst* (*Utolenie zhazhdy*).

The characters in *Slaking the Thirst*, a somewhat schematic novel à *thèse*, serve as mouthpieces for distinct points of view. Much as *Students* mirrors the atmosphere of its period, *Slaking the Thirst* reflects the hopes kindled by the Khrushchev revelations of 1956. The "thirst" of the title refers both to the physical thirst felt by those working in the desert and to the metaphoric thirst for truth and justice felt by Soviet citizens in the years after Khrushchev's secret speech at the Twentieth Party Congress. Trifonov neither disguises nor encodes the metaphor. During an argument about the "proper" way to quench thirst, for example, one character advises following the Turkic example of offering small sips of water to someone returning from the desert; too much water at once would be harmful, he contends. "That's nonsense!" retorts another. "I don't believe it! ... How can there be too much truth? Or too much justice?"

Individuals in *Slaking the Thirst* are mainly passive, acted upon by the times rather than taking action themselves. They exert very little countervailing force. Still, Trifonov avoids simplistic categories of "positive" and "negative" polarities, and even his least sympathetic characters give some evidence of complexity of motivation. Time, which later became a flowing, plastic element in his prose, consists here of discrete moments lacking a past and merely hopeful of a future.

In 1965 Trifonov published *The Campfire's Glow* (*Otblesk kostra*), a book made possible by the Khrushchev thaw. Again we read an account of a loving but threatened childhood. The child recalls his closeness to his father when they made kites and flew them on the bank of the river. At the same time the child recalls a sense of fear: the loving intimacy is menaced. That imminent deprivation, which shadows the happy childhood of some character in every work Trifonov wrote, is important not merely as a clue to Trifonov's own emotional development. It is a feature of his biography that he shared with readers of his own postrevolutionary generation, especially readers of similar urban revolutionary background.[11]

Even in *Students*, which was written when no mention of the purges was possible, Trifonov deprived his young hero of a father, using the transparent (if plausible) device of a war casualty. The sequence recurs in book after book: happy childhood is abruptly destroyed in 1937–38 when the parents disappear; the father will never return; the family is evicted from their central, comfortable apartment and relocated to an outlying region of Moscow, where the grandmother functions in loco parentis.

If the destroyed childhood in *The Campfire's Glow* was known territory, in other ways the book broke new ground for Trifonov. The subtitle, *A Documentary Novella*, suggests Trifonov's approach. Out of documents—pages from his uncle's diary, his father's letters, official papers—Trifonov attempted to reconstruct an era, or rather a turbulent history stretching from 1904 to 1937, using the past of his own family. On his mother's side, his was a family of staunch supporters of the Bolsheviks and committed party members. Trifonov's maternal grandmother, Slovatinskaia, joined the Communist party in 1904; her son, Trifonov's uncle Pavel Lur'e, joined the party as a fourteen-year-old student in Petrograd in 1917 and kept a detailed diary that Trifonov made extensive use of in both *The Campfire's Glow* and the considerably later novel *The Old Man*.

Trifonov's political and ideological legacy from his father was equally clear-cut. His father, Valentin, whom he described as a "born organizer" and "professional revolutionary," joined the party in 1904, along with his older brother; Valentin was then sixteen years old. Both teenagers were involved in the 1905 revolt in Rostov, for which Valentin was sentenced to administrative exile in Siberia. Rearrested in his exile site, the city of Tiumen, for revolutionary work, he spent three more years in exile, eventually returning to Petersburg. After the February revolution he was elected secretary of the Bolshevik faction of the Petrograd Soviet of Worker-Deputies and was one of the organizers of the Red Guard.

The Campfire's Glow was Trifonov's first literary attempt to come to grips with his father's history, which encapsulated in one individual life the history of a whole generation of revolutionaries. The novella depicts the political events of that history without mining their implications. Trifonov outlines the fate of the Cossack Civil War Corps commander Filip Mironov, for instance, in The Campfire's Glow, but it was another ten years before he scrutinized that fate, and his own family's involvement in it, in The Old Man.

In The Campfire's Glow Trifonov confronts his father's ghost, discharging what he clearly perceived as an obligation to his father's life. The confrontation seemingly liberated him to pose certain moral issues he had evaded previously, for a new focus and purpose is evident in his work after The Campfire's Glow. The book was equally important artistically, thanks to Trifonov's experimentation with time montages and multiple narrative voice. The action of Campfire's Glow moves freely from decade to decade, its episodes connected internally rather than by serial chronology. The third-person narration is mainly unadorned and matter-of-fact, but the use of documents allows Trifonov to modulate intonations. His father's dry, uninflected voice—the voice of the organizer, thoughtfully summing up the revolution in theory and practice—emerges from articles and reports, while personal letters speak far more emotionally, often expressing frustration and anger with the ham-handed and even dangerously short-sighted tactics of those who would advance the ideals of the revolution. In addition to Valentin Trifonov's "voices," there is a narrator who is neither participant nor even witness, but something like a historian. "This voice is epic, distanced from reality. It speaks after the event."[12]

Trifonov wrote The Campfire's Glow in the milder, hopeful climate of Khrushchev's reign. Many writers were similarly encouraged. Those were the years in which Evgeniia Ginzburg wrote the first volume of her memoirs, *Journey into the Whirlwind*, with every intention of publishing it; indeed, the book ends with encomia to the "new day" which has finally come. In that "new day" Roi Medvedev wrote his history of Stalinism, *Let History Judge*, and his brother Zhores wrote his investigation of the Lysenko affair; the historian Aleksandr Nekrich completed his study of Stalin's lack of preparedness for war in 1941. All of them (and many others) had reason to hope that their works would be available to readers within the Soviet Union. As it turned out, by the time they were ready to go to press, publication was no longer possible.[13]

By the time *The Campfire's Glow* appeared, the Khrushchev era with its limited openness was over. The years that followed were troubled and repressive—times of literary and political trials. In the mid-1960s Trifonov was able to publish several stories, albeit with some difficulty. One of them, "Pigeon Death" (*Golubinaia gibel'*), deserves special attention, both for its publishing history and for its allusive treatment of the immediate post-Stalin period.

"Pigeon Death" was submitted to *Novyi mir* in 1966 together with two other stories. The others appeared that same year, while "Pigeon Death" was published only after a two-year delay. Even then, the issue (number 1, January 1968) was held back until March while editor Aleksandr Tvardovskii fought for permission to print Solzhenitsyn's *Cancer Ward*. In the end, *Cancer Ward* was blocked by the censors; Trifonov's story, despite its pessimistic ending, may have been a substitute.[14]

The story is set in 1954, the year after Stalin's death, and therefore significant. An elderly husband and wife living in a communal apartment are forced to get rid of the pigeons they have been feeding and tending in order to placate complaining neighbors. The old man carries the pigeons to a different location and sets them free there, but they return to their habitual perch. He eventually has no choice but to kill them. The story is a strong, if indirect, indictment of a system, and an era, that sacrificed individuals to selfishness and material success. The well-dressed woman who harasses the couple is a representative of the "new class"—self-important, arrogant, and powerful; the symbol of authority in the story, the building superintendent, is an officious and amoral character who terrorizes the tenants. By means of differentiated speech levels Trifonov re-creates the Soviet social hierarchy: the elderly husband and wife talk to each other and to their *kommunalka* neighbors in casual, relaxed language, but they answer the superintendent formally and use overly respectful, almost obsequious, language with the "lady." The anti-Semitic campaign of the early 1950s is alluded to in the arrest of one man, the father of a sickly girl, and in the consequent eviction of the girl and her mother and grandmother from the communal apartment.[15]

Hard on the heels of "Pigeon Death" came the first of the three novellas that comprise the Moscow trilogy. In these novellas—*The Exchange* (*Obmen*; 1969), *Taking Stock* (*Predvaritel'nye itogi*; 1970), and *The Long Goodbye* (*Dolgoe proshchanie*; 1971)—familiar thematic conflicts are shifted into new contexts, with different emphases. The critical reception that greeted the novellas was characteristic of the political-cultural context in which Trifonov wrote and to which he was forced to respond.

Two of the three novellas are set in modern Moscow, with flashbacks to the early 1950s; the third, *The Long Goodbye*, is set almost entirely in the early 1950s, although its action is framed by the "present" of 1970. In each, the hero faces a moral crossroads; in each, petty bourgeois values (*meshchanstvo*) oppose the values of the intelligentsia. In *The Exchange* and *Taking Stock* Trifonov portrays an urbanized Soviet society that has become dominated by the *meshchanstvo*; in *The Long Goodbye* he shows the roots of that transformation, which occurred as the ideals of the intelligentsia withered.

Dmitriev, the protagonist of *The Exchange*, is facing the imminent death of his mother, Ksenia Fedorovna. His wife, Lena, wants her to move in with them so that they can eventually obtain a larger apartment. This innocent-seeming proposition, to which Dmitriev ultimately acquiesces, represents the culmination of a series of moral choices, an exchange of one set of values for the other that began in the early 1950s. The values are associated with the two families: Lena's petty bourgeois parents (the Lukianovs), and Dmitriev's grandfather, mother, and sister, all members of the revolutionary and postrevolutionary intelligentsia.

Trifonov is evenhanded in portraying the two clans and the positive and negative aspects of both value systems. Lena's unattractive traits—insensitivity, ambition, material greed—coexist with genuine devotion to her family and considerable cleverness. Dmitriev's mother, Ksenia Fedorovna, seems at first reading to be an advertisement for the principled ideals of the intelligentsia. But she insists too often on her humility to be entirely convincing, her pride in her family's past is complacent and condescending, and her altruism is, as her son acknowledges, sometimes tainted by self-consciousness. Trifonov later commented that Ksenia Fedorovna commanded his sympathy less because of her personality or values than because she was dying.[16]

It is apparent in *The Exchange* that notwithstanding Trifonov's acknowledgment of the Lukianovs' "virtues," Lena and her family are fundamentally alien to Trifonov, while the Dmitrievs are known and loved. The Dmitrievs' flaws, acknowledged by Trifonov both explicitly and tacitly, are the faults of "his" kind of family, if not indeed of his own family. Between the earliest action of the novel (the remembered courtship and marriage of Dmitriev and Lena in May 1954) and the end of the work in August 1968, the whole country has become "Lukianovized"—that is, has adopted the selfish, materialistic, self-serving values of Lena's parents and has turned its back on its own history.

The decay of Soviet society is shown most clearly in the Lukianovs' indifference toward Dmitriev's grandfather, a former revolutionary. He returns to Moscow from what we understand to be a number of years in the Gulag, though Trifonov never identifies it as such. This dignified Old Bolshevik is, to the Lukianovs, no more than a relic of former times and quite irrelevant to their lives. Dmitriev loves him, but he too is Lukianovized: en route to his grandfather's funeral he stops to buy some cans of fish that Lena loves, and throughout the funeral his attention is divided between his grandfather and the fish, as he makes a mental note not to leave it behind.

If Dmitriev is shown in the process of betraying a certain set of values, his successor, the ailing protagonist of *Taking Stock*, has already betrayed them.[17] Gennadii Sergeevich is suffering the consequences of twenty years of compromise. A translator by profession, he has fled Moscow for Turkmenia, ostensibly for business reasons but actually in order to escape an intolerable family crisis. Many of Trifonov's heroes flee from Moscow when they perceive it as a sterile environment, in attempts at romantic rebellion. Often they run to the barren deserts of central Asia, but they always return. Whatever apartment they happen to live in, Moscow is their real home, protective yet not demanding.[18] The city, like its famous street the Arbat in Bulat Okudzhava's song, is their "profession . . . religion . . . fatherland."

Like Dmitriev, Gennadii Sergeevich is married to a woman of undeniable gifts, but she has allowed them to atrophy. She is an idle and pretentious woman, and she treats her husband with an impatience only occasionally tempered by affection. Their teenaged son, Kiril, has broken the law and feels no guilt; worse, he has stolen from his selfless, vulnerable old nanny but feels no remorse.

All three characters individually, and the family as a unit, are spoiled and selfish, morally degraded. Only Gennadii Sergeevich, though he is weak and self-indulgent (one critic labeled him a "pathetic failure"),[19] realizes what they have lost and accepts some of his own responsibility for that loss. He chose to leave his first wife for Rita. He passively tolerated the growing corruption of his own home. He did not prevent the exploitation of the old nanny; more, he abetted it. Yet because he has some understanding of his guilt, he alone has the potential to redeem the family. Indeed, as the novella closes, Trifonov sends him back to Moscow from central Asia, giving him a second chance to evince some "everyday heroism."[20]

Both Dmitriev and Gennadii Sergeevich married and embarked on their careers in the early 1950s, at the end of the Stalin years. They didn't realize then that the choices they were making would set up patterns for their entire adult lives, nor did they perceive a social context which approved, if it did not dictate, those choices. In *The Long Goodbye* Trifonov re-creates the societal context in which such choices were shaped and validated. The sources of what ripens into Dmitriev's moral lassitude and Gennadii Sergeevich's corruption are patent in the choices made by the main characters in *The Long Goodbye*: Lialia, her common-law husband, Grisha Rebrov, and her lover, Smolianov.

When *The Long Goodbye* opens, Lialia is an unsuccessful actress on tour with her acting company in a provincial city. They are performing a play by a local author, Smolianov, who hosts a party for the actors after the performance. Lialia's colleagues make fun of him, while not scrupling to feast on the food his mother has so painstakingly prepared. Lialia feels sorry for him at the party, and the night ends with their making love.

Though their affair begins spontaneously and without thought of profit, it becomes a matter of calculation on both sides, and Lialia becomes a star in her company thanks to Smolianov's patronage. Smolianov is shown to be a decent man at first, if a playwright of small talent. As he profits from the corruption endemic to the period, however, he loses his original simplicity and integrity. And Grisha, a would-be playwright, is not much better, despite being an *intelligent* of urban revolutionary background and the first of what became in Trifonov's subsequent works a series of "historian-heroes." He enjoys the fruits of Lialia's success, thanks to a carefully maintained blindness to what is really happening, until he can no longer escape knowledge of her infidelity, and then he runs away.

In keeping with Trifonov's refusal to affix simplistic labels to his characters, all three combine unlovely qualities with admirable traits. Grisha, standard-bearer of the values of the intelligentsia, is selfish and irresponsible toward Lialia. He despises the vulgarity exemplified by Lialia's mother, among others, but he contents himself with expressing his contempt and keeping himself apart from it. Lialia herself is a mixture of ambition, greed, devotion, and compassion. Smolianov goes from innocent enjoyment of his success to cynical exploitation of it—yet he also has a retarded daughter whom he loves dearly and a mentally ill wife for whom he feels responsible.

The intellectual and artistic climate of the period, never explicitly designated as Stalinist, provides the subtext for the novella. Grisha's historical inquiries concentrate on rebels and dissenters, a focus highly suspect in the acute conformism of late-Stalinist Russia, even though "his" dissenters lived in tsarist Russia. Whenever he discusses it with friends and professional contacts, they roundly discourage him from pursuing the subject.[21]

The postwar repressions that affected all of Soviet culture were particularly hard on the theater. One of Zhdanov's infamous decrees in the summer of 1946 dealt specifically with "the repertoire of dramatic theaters," adding to already onerous regulations the requirement that each theater stage "at least two new spectacles of high ideological and artistic quality on Soviet contemporary themes." Such demands, in combination with the theory of "no-conflict" drama and the reduced autonomy of artistic personnel, created a theatrical climate fatal to any kind of originality and quality.[22] In the character of Smolianov, Trifonov portrays a playwright of that era, swept to success not because of his talents, which are minimal, but because he writes plays that satisfy current political *cum* cultural demands.

The death of Stalin averted what many feared would be a new wave of terror. Stalin's death is alluded to at the end of the main text of *The Long Goodbye*, when Grisha takes a train out of Moscow to escape the intolerable emotional crisis produced by Lialia's betrayal and abortion. Passengers whisper meaningfully about a death that has just occurred, and the scene concludes with the question "Will it be different now?"

Despite the hopeful onset of a new era, the effects of the long night are not so easily shrugged off. The answer provided by the epilogue, set seventeen years after the main action, is ambiguous: life is different, but the differences grow out of what has already occurred. Grisha has abandoned his historical research to become a successful writer, while Lialia has given up acting, a profession she greatly loved, for marriage and a child. Trifonov intimates that Lialia has settled placidly into her life as a *meshchanka*, and that Grisha's *intelligentnost'* has been swallowed up by the compromises demanded as the price of success.

Trifonov's trilogy encountered no serious prepublication problems. It did, however, provoke objections from Soviet critics, especially the more orthodox ones. Using categories of judgment dating from the postwar period, they berated Trifonov for the "hermetic" quality of the trilogy: that is, its inattention to the advances made by the larger society. One typical comment describes the world of Trifonov's Moscow characters as one "of egotistic self-will and base instincts," while Trifonov ignores the "big world of communist transformation and revolutionary morality."[23] Trifonov was branded a *bytopisatel'*, a writer of the everyday, preoccupied with the detritus of quotidian reality to the exclusion of more "important" matters and more significant themes; he was rebuked for portraying women who have affairs either because they have romantic illusions about sex or because they are afraid of aging.[24]

On aesthetic grounds Trifonov was faulted for an authorial stance that was interpreted as disinterested. He failed explicitly to

condemn those characters who ought—in the view of many critics—to be condemned. Even sympathetic readers accused Trifonov
of fence-sitting. Lev Anninskii, for instance, a sensitive interpreter
and consistent partisan of Trifonov's work, felt that the very aesthetic of the trilogy, the "confident and consistent style" of the
novellas, demanded judgment, the "decisive resolution of problems."
Its absence—what Anninskii called "authorial uncertainty"—undermined the works, destroying their structural integrity.[25]

The critical attention devoted to Trifonov's trilogy tacitly acknowledged that he had begun a new phase in his writing, an
impression enhanced by *Another Life* (1975), which is often discussed in concert with the novellas. In between, Trifonov published
a long historical novel, *Impatience* (*Neterpenie*; 1973), part of a series
of books on the Russian revolutionary past to which many prominent writers contributed. In plot and setting *Impatience* is a clear
departure from the *bytovaia* prose of the trilogy. Thematically, however, it functions as a bridge between the post-Stalinist Soviet "present" depicted in the trilogy and *Another Life*, and the seeds of that
present in the Russian and Soviet past.

Impatience is a treatment of the idealistic young radicals of the
1870s and 1880s, in particular the People's Will group (*narodnaia
volia*) which ultimately engaged in terrorist activities. Trifonov himself considered the novel a statement against the efficacy of terror:
"I tried to show that true social goals cannot be attained with the
help of terror."[26] The relationship between ends and means fasci-
nated Trifonov, as did the questions of political morality implied
by it. *Impatience* provided a safe context in which to examine them,
in that its events are distanced by a century's time and by the idealism motivating the group, if ultimately misdirected by its leaders.

Within a few years Trifonov took the risk of moving into the
Soviet period, so that in light of his later work *Impatience* seems a
prologue for his discussions of political morality during the Russian
Civil War (in *The Old Man*) and the Stalinist years (*House on the
Embankment* and *Time and Place*). At the time, however, it was considered a fairly conventional glorification of the precursors of the
Russian Revolution. One Swiss reviewer, in fact, read *Impatience* as
a Marxist reproach to those who rely upon individual deeds without
having a mass base; he criticized Trifonov's "evasion" of historical

analysis, which ignored the untenable and unjust nature of the rebels' actions by restricting the book to their perspective.[27]

Back squarely in the modern world, *Another Life* (1975) shares with the Moscow novellas its contemporary Moscow setting, its detailed everyday texture, and its repetition and development of certain themes. Its basic relationships, both those between individuals and those between value systems, are familiar. Many character types are recognizable, though the hero, Sergei Troitskii, shows an occasional buffoonery unusual in Trifonov's fiction. *Another Life* has a consistently female perspective, for virtually the entire book is told from the point of view of the newly widowed Olga Vasilievna, who obsessively traces her life with her husband Sergei to understand what it was like, what he was like, what went wrong, and why he died.

Another Life sparked a lively critical debate. Sergei appealed to many readers as an attractive seeker-after-truth, a historian who suffers as a result of his unwillingness to compromise intellectually and whose early death is caused, in part, by the stresses and pressures to which his morally more elastic colleagues subject him. Many readers perceived Sergei as the true protagonist of the novel, despite Olga's dominant voice, and as a spokesman for Trifonov.[28] Others saw him as a weak and passive character, and Olga as a shrew who drove him to his death: "The one had no luck within her family, the other failed both with his family and at work." Their unhappiness stems from their inhumanity toward one another, their stupidity, and their desire to give pain.[29] Yet their unhappiness coexists with genuine love and intimacy, especially a strong sexual bond.[30] Olga's despair comes from feeling bereft of that intimacy as well as from guilt. The intolerable feeling that she herself is to blame for Sergei's death generates her aggression, a search for "guilty parties" in which her memory defensively picks out all the ways in which Sergei's life was poisoned by colleagues at his institute.[31]

As Anatolii Bocharov says, neither Sergei nor Olga can be "reduced to a single formula." The two are "antipodes and twins," victims and creators of their own mutual misunderstanding, separated by a mutual spiritual deafness. Sergei's thirst for independence clashes with the "despotism" of Olga's love.[32] More is at stake than clashing emotional needs: "It is not just the torment of mutual incomprehension of the most intimate people, the dramatic leitmotif of all of Trifonov's work from *The Exchange* on. The conflict here is of fundamental beliefs, of worldviews and outlooks on life."[33]

Trifonov understood both outlooks. In *Another Life* he transmits Olga's positivist, materialist views, which affirm and advance life. He rewards her for her faith in life by freeing her, ultimately, from her pain and guilt. He even grants her "another" life: a new love, new energy, and happiness. Olga is no malign philistine: her worldview may be narrower than her husband's, but her point of view is defended with what occasionally verges on eloquence, and her constricting jealousy springs from a deep love for Sergei. Nonetheless, Trifonov's fundamental sympathies lie with Sergei, his historian-hero who cannot manage to compromise even when he tries to, and who masks his pain with an overdeveloped sense of mischief.

Another Life is the first of what one critic has called "remembrance-contemplations" (*vospominaniia-razmyshleniia*): "not childhood but recollections of childhood, not love but the memory of love, not mistakes but their retrospective analysis."[34] Memory becomes subject as well as the means of recall: private memory in Olga's reconstruction of her life with Sergei, and societal memory in Sergei's fascination with history and his passion to pursue research in unsanctioned directions. Sergei, a character created four years after Grisha Rebrov in *The Long Goodbye*, is a historian by profession, not merely by avocation. The problems he has at his institute are directly related to his view of history and to his refusal to compromise or corrupt his own research. What in Grisha Rebrov was simply one facet of his character, however revealing an aspect, becomes in Sergei the prism through which he understands the world and through which we in turn must understand him.

In *Another Life*, and in each work that followed it, the past is Trifonov's subject, one he often shares with his hero. In each novel the past is seen partially through the screen of the present, which may be relegated to the wings, as it is in *House on the Embankment*, or may share the stage with the past, as it does in *The Old Man*. In each of Trifonov's later works the Soviet past is presented in a much more complex relationship with the characters' lives than it is in the coded presentations of Trifonov's earlier works, including *Another Life*. The past, then, is the logical next step in this study.

Themes

II

Young Men

With the fall of Khrushchev, officially sanctioned thaws gave way to officially mandated repressions. Particularly after the 1966 trial of authors Andrei Siniavskii and Iulii Daniel and the 1968 invasion of Czechoslovakia, the hopes of liberals faded and their anticipation of a serious reexamination of the Soviet past foundered. By 1968 the message emanating from official quarters was clear: the Stalinist chapter was considered closed.

Paradoxically, precisely at the time his society moved into a period of greater repression, Trifonov initiated, and insistently pursued, a greater openness in his work. The Moscow novellas of 1969, 1970, and 1971 expose the anomie and soullessness of modern Soviet society. They were succeeded by four books—*Another Life*, *House on the Embankment*, *The Old Man*, and *Time and Place*—which look backward, to the Soviet past. Trifonov turned his attention to the roots of modern disaffection, roots he perceived as squarely and deeply planted in the soil of Soviet history.

Trifonov's work suggests that he was slow to move from the present to the Stalin years, and slow to connect Stalinism with Leninism, even by implication. He was perhaps slower than many of his peers, either from calculation or from genuine uncertainty. Once having begun, however, he steadily traced threads backward: to Stalin's death, to the anticosmopolitan campaign, to the Terror, and back to the Civil War and its violence, both White and Red. In the words of one Soviet critic, Trifonov "could no longer [write] without the verticals: the pure present had ceased to exist for him."[1]

Trifonov's work offers two fundamentally different, though not mutually exclusive, patterns of reclaiming the past for present understanding. One is reconstructive, a process of accretion that stitches together bits and pieces, shards of events and memories. The other is deconstructive, a process of excavation that Sergei, in *Another Life*, dubs "graverobbing," and Letunov, in *The Old Man*, sees as "stripping off bloody bandages." Often it requires deciphering, as a kind of national and personal palimpsest. Everyday life—which in Trifonov's early work is chiefly a re-creation of external reality— now becomes an aesthetic means rather than an end in itself. It does not simply provide the context of his characters' choices; it is part of the choices themselves, part of his characters' psyches. Modern Soviet urban society becomes the topsoil of his fiction, shifted aside, spadeful by spadeful, to lay bare its roots in the past.

Roots

Trifonov's abiding and profound need to examine Russian history is everywhere manifest. It is apparent in his first examination of his father's and uncle's lives—the 1966 documentary novel *The Campfire's Glow*—and in his choice of the People's Will movement as the subject of *Impatience*. He was not alone in his concern. Even before the legitimation of historical investigation ushered in by *glasnost'* in late 1985 and 1986, Soviet fiction of the 1970s revealed a preoccupation with the past, with memory, and with the ethical consequences of forgetting the past.[2] The eminent Academician and medievalist Dmitri Likhachev calls memory "the force which opposes the destructive force of time": without memory there can be no conscience.[3] Chingiz Aitmatov, whose own novels and plays reveal connections between the past and the present, explains the need for a profound vision of the past, exemplified in a contemporary literary preoccupation with folkloric motifs and images, as partly an attempt to understand the personality in the context of past eras and partly a belief that legends, myths, and songs may help to reveal this multifaceted reality.[4] The Soviet critic Natalia Ivanova notes the unlikely popularity of scholarly books relating to memory and the past, as well as memoirs and a best-seller called *Literary Heritage*;[5] and Western scholars have remarked the same trends, pointing to the work of architectural historians like N. N. Voronin; the large editions of guidebooks to Vladimir-Suzdal, Novgorod, and other landmarks of pre-Petrine Russia and especially the Russian Orthodox church; the publication in *Novyi mir* of essays on scholarly expeditions into the countryside; and the substantial number of books on iconography and folk art.[6]

Trifonov belongs to this powerful and enduring tradition. He is always most sympathetic toward those characters who have some kind of interest in the past, endowing even secondary characters, such as Anton in *House on the Embankment* and the schoolmaster Slaboserdov in *The Old Man*, with an awareness of history's importance. He shares his own preoccupation with history with his heroes, though their attitude and understanding often differ from his own. Letunov, the elderly retired engineer of *The Old Man*, is obsessed with the years of the Civil War. Grisha Rebrov, the hapless writer in *Long Goodbye*, makes a meager living writing "parables" and plays about Korea but reserves his real passion for nineteenth-century Russian history. His enthusiasms are scattered among the Decembrists, Nechaev, Nechaev's "tool" Pryzhov (involved in the murder of Ivanov), the uprising of Polish exiles in Siberia, the People's Will members, and a double agent of theirs, Kletochnikov, who ostensibly worked for the notorious Third Section (the tsarist secret police). Sasha Antipov, the novelist-hero of Trifonov's last novel, *Time and Place*, grapples with a manuscript that penetrates deep into the Russian past by means of a series of mirror-imaged lives. Beginning with the novel's contemporary protagonist, Nikiforov, Antipov's book stretches back to the eighteenth century. Even Vadim Glebov, who comes closest to an antihero among Trifonov's protagonists and who makes every effort to expunge his own past, chooses as his dissertation topic the journalism of the 1880s. Trifonov's interest in the past is neither sentimental nor undifferentiated: his characters examine those epochs and historical facts which prefigure the fate of their own generation, as does he.

Grisha Rebrov speaks for Trifonov in an argument with Smolianov about Russia's past. The issue is *pochva*, a term that literally means "soil" but also encompasses national and spiritual roots and often refers exclusively to rural peasant roots. Smolianov attributes Grisha's flounderings and failures to his lack of rootedness in Russian *pochva*. Grisha angrily wonders which "soil" precisely Smolianov has in mind: "The *chernozem* [black earth]? The *podzol* [sterile, salt-deficient soil]? Fertilized soil? My soil is that of historical experience—everything that Russia has lived and suffered through!" (*LG* 276). Like Grisha, Trifonov rejected Smolianov's view of the Russian past. Trifonov saw Russia as a country with a revolutionary tradition of intelligentsia and working-class people. The peasantry, although important, was only one part of its population, and not necessarily the best and most central part. For Trifonov, exaggeration of the peasant role to the virtual exclusion of the intelligentsia and workers smacked of historical absurdity as well as of neo-Slavophilism. Though Trifonov never said so, it was Stalin who demanded the glorification of the peasantry. Smolianov's mediocre plays fulfill this demand, hence his success.[7]

Grisha's historical interests focus on the People's Will participants, the *narodniki*, for much the same reason as Trifonov's did in *Impatience*: they were idealists who resorted to terror in the service of their ideals. To at least some extent, therefore, they prefigured the revolutionaries of 1917. From an entirely understandable rage at the inequities and injustices of the system, the *narodniki* proceeded to use means that were destructive both of their cause and of their personal integrity. Trifonov insisted on distinguishing expedience from necessity, demarcating Nechaev—and Nechaev's definition of morality as "whatever helps the revolution"—from Andrei Zheliabov and the People's Will members, who despite their final recourse to acts of terrorism were horrified by the possibility that bystanders might die. Nechaev's sole program, Trifonov wrote in an article on Dostoevskii, was destruction, while the *narodniki* did not reject a Christian understanding of goodness, comradeship, and so on.[8]

Grisha is intrigued by Kletochnikov, the double agent, and his chameleonlike negative capability. What makes Kletochnikov's deceit successful is, Grisha thinks, his lack of any distinctive qualities. That type of personality seems best suited to become a conduit: "He [Kletochnikov] had nothing, nothing at all. He was an instrument. He carried out the will of others, which some called the people's will" (*LG* 316). In another time, in other circumstances, such a man without qualities becomes Vadim Glebov, the protagonist of *House on the Embankment*; he too carries out the will of others, which "some called the 'people's will.'"

Grisha Rebrov's research into Russian history is limited both by the times he lives in and by what, in 1971, Trifonov himself was prepared to examine. Four years later, in *Another Life*, Trifonov went further, creating as his hero a professional historian—the only professional historian among his main characters. For Sergei Troitskii the past both forms and informs his life in the present: it both shapes and grows out of his character. Sergei has Trifonov's own understanding of history as being "present in every day, in each human fate. It layers—broadly, invisibly, sometimes even in distinctly visible deposits—everything which goes toward forming contemporaneity.... The past exists as much in the future as it does in the present."[9] Sergei's worldview is conditioned by his conception of the past as living into the present and the future through individuals. His problems at the institute are directly related to his view of history and his refusal to compromise his own research. Some of the tension in his marriage stems from the fundamental incompatibility between his attitude toward investigating the past and the views held by his wife.

Threads

Like Grisha, Sergei Troitskii is unsuccessful. For him, as for Grisha, the study of history becomes a narcotic, often random and undirected, sometimes pointless, but addictive. And again like Grisha, Sergei articulates many of Trifonov's own feelings about history and about the relationship between past and present.[10] His perpetual search for the connections is a lonely one; even his loving wife does not understand it, though she tries. His colleagues' interpretation of history is self-referential and calculating, his mother's is sterile. Tatiana Patera has observed that Sergei shares a problem with Grisha: both devote passionate study to complex moments of Russian and Soviet history, moments about which there already exists a "proper" point of view in official historiography. With Sergei it is the years of the Fourth Duma (November 1912–February 1917), when the Bolsheviks and Mensheviks fought bitterly. (Like Grisha, Sergei's interests range: he worked first on the history of the streets of Moscow, then on the Okhrana, then the February Revolution.) Sergei's colleagues at the institute are unenthusiastic about his work. Personal ambition apart, they are concerned that he will come upon double agents among Communist party activists in the teens of this century who were actually working for the tsarist police. Such discoveries, violating the iconic image of Bolshevik purity, would be especially unwelcome in 1967, the fiftieth anniversary year of the revolution.[11]

Furthermore, Sergei's theory of historical continuity and the method of investigation he derives from it are, within his intellectual and political milieu, decidedly suspect. His semifacetious catchword, "searching out the threads" (otyskivanie nitei), conceals an approach to history whose goal is the demythologizing of the past, the recovery of its true image from under layers of greasepaint.[12] His "grave robbing" (razryvanie mogil) echoes Herzen, who wrote that man "wants to be neither a passive grave-digger of the past, nor the unconscious midwife of the future."[13]

Sergei's philosophy of history—and, consequently, his morality—derives loosely from Herzen's insistence on the possibility of free human action and choice. In his dispute with his onetime schoolmate Klimuk, Sergei pits his interpretation against a crude determinism that makes a mockery of ethics. Klimuk, now Sergei's superior at the institute, is a generally unscrupulous type, as we see in his willingness to pander for (as well as to) his boss when they visit Sergei's dacha. But it is his stance toward the past that most blatantly characterizes his amorality. For Klimuk, history—what actually happened and why—is secondary. "Nothing is important or means anything except historical expediency [istoricheskaia tselesoobraznost']," he says. Sergei vehemently disagrees: historical expediency is "something indistinct and treacherous [rasplyvchatoe i kovarnoe], like a swamp." Who defines it? he asks rhetorically, and answers sardonically, "The Academic Council, by majority vote?" (AL 275–76).[14]

Klimuk is an arrogant and egotistic careerist; Sergei is self-indulgent and weak. There is no grandeur in modern Moscow; there are no Soviet equivalents of Ivan Karamazov and the Grand Inquisitor. Yet neither the defects of individual personalities nor the triviality of the context should mask the gravity of the issues. Is history open, thus implying freedom and imposing responsibility on men? Or is it closed, obeying what Herzen called an "inevitable plan ... in which men are willy-nilly involved," in which case "nothing can be vicious or cruel or stupid or ugly that is a means to the fulfillment of the objectively given cosmic purpose."[15] In the words of Isaiah Berlin, "The chasm between Herzen and Bakunin is not bridgeable."[16]

Sergei comes upon a list of names of secret informers from the second decade of the century. Klimuk first implies that it is a forgery, and then he tries to persuade Sergei to turn it over to another researcher. Presumably the list is authentic, or it wouldn't be in such demand; even after Sergei's death the representative from the institute who pays a condolence call on Olga makes sure to ask her to look for it. But the only reason such men as Klimuk want the list is for the use, or abuse, they can make of it. They may not plan to destroy it, but they will certainly not respect its integrity, because their interest lies not in history but in historical expediency.

A similarly instrumentalist view of the past emerges in the conversation between Sergei's mother, Aleksandra Prokofievna, and Klimuk. Irritated by Klimuk's success (and her son's relative failure) and wanting to take him down a peg or two, she reminds him of his brother's onetime criminal activities. Klimuk, equally irritated, snaps back at her, "Listen, this is theater of the absurd! . . . My God, why bring all that up now—why should I, or you, or anybody? . . . There is such a concept as historical expediency. . . . Do you know who my brother is now?" (AL 274).

Klimuk would like to manipulate the past in the service of the present, especially in the service of his own ambitions. Others, less venal, are equally ready to jettison the past out of more pragmatic motives—as the sensible thing to do—or for the sake of simplicity. In the culturally repressive atmosphere of the late 1940s and early 1950s, Olga's artist stepfather dissociated himself from the modernist artists who were his friends in the 1920s. He burned his own nonrealistic paintings, but a print of *Guernica* still adorns his wall. (In his late story "Visit to Marc Chagall" Trifonov retells this "anecdote," identifying the suspect picture as a self-portrait by Chagall.) His brother Petia chides him: "They gave it to you for formalism, George-boy [*tebia, Egorsha, luptsevali*], but I guess not enough. Why do you have junk like that on your walls?" (AL 237). Pantiusha, the grandson of Sergei's double agent, is confused by too complex a view of the past. He shouts at Sergei: "The hell with you historians! . . . We learned all this history in school. We know it! What are you mixing me up for [*mozgi pudrite*]? History, history. . . . Enough, there's only one history and we don't need any more!" (*AL* 314). Eventually Pantiusha comes to like Sergei, but he never seems persuaded by Sergei's arguments or impressed by his claim that history "belongs" to everyone.

What can easily be forgiven in Pantiusha, and understood in Petia, is harder to accept in the case of Aleksandra Prokofievna, Sergei's mother. As a Red Army *Politotdel* worker in 1920, she was herself a "maker of history" (*delatel'nitsa istorii*), and she does not turn her back on the past. On the contrary, she frequently recalls it, measuring the present by its yardstick. In fact, she is unable to move into the present; she cannot incorporate and revise her youthful experiences in the light of what followed. Her memories have become a source not of understanding but of intolerance. In her attempts to control others—her son, her daughter-in-law, her granddaughter—she wields the past like a sword. Olga's fantasy captures the essence of her mother-in-law: the room is transformed into a phantom tribunal of the 1920s, with her mother-in-law presiding, lacking only a commissar's leather jacket and a Mauser in a wooden holster.[17]

Indeed, when Sergei's dissertation is rejected, his mother sounds like the *agitprop* spokeswoman she was nearly half a century before: the more criticism he receives, the better his work will be in the end. At your age, she says sternly, we never worried about money; the only people who did worry were private traders and grasping peasants and those who had lost their property in the revolution. Inappropriately, she applies a self-created myth of the past to the realities of the present. Her inapt reproaches to her granddaughter Irinka—who wants to buy shoes on the black market—are similarly rooted in a mythicized past.

Essentially Aleksandra Prokofievna is at fault for using the past as a kind of stencil to be laid over the present. She enshrines and freezes the past; she does not learn from it. (She shares this quality with a number of women characters who are modeled on Trifonov's maternal grandmother: Dmitriev's mother in *The Exchange*, Ganchuk's wife in *House on the Embankment*, Gorik's grandmother in *The Disappearance*.) She "turns principle into dogma, reduces everything to black-and-white schemes."[18] When she and Sergei argue about his fascination with parapsychology, her son pinpoints the problem:

"And you, Mama, have remained completely untouched by that time [the passage of forty years]. In its own way quite an accomplishment" (AL 344).

It is in the character of Olga that Trifonov most sympathetically limns an alternative to Sergei's concept of history. Olga is by nature a pragmatist. She appreciates her stepfather's Picasso print no more than her uncle Petia or her mother-in-law. She is as irritated as Klimuk by her mother-in-law's pointless recollection of Klimuk's criminal brother ("Why dig up ancient history," she thinks), although in Olga's case it is because she is afraid it might backfire and hurt Sergei. Her pragmatism, which occasionally blurs into calculation, combines with a fiercely possessive love for Sergei, leading her to reject the past, to reject anything that preceded her life with Sergei. Thus she is impatient of Sergei's "naïve" attachment (her phrase) to his old schoolfriends: "All men have this strange trait. They can't live without old buddies. Whereas Olga Vasilievna could get along very well without girlfriends once Serezha was on the scene, she could go for months without seeing Faina or anyone else" (AL 265). (Although written in the technical third person, as if these are the conclusions of an omniscient narrator, Trifonov is in fact conveying Olga's thoughts.) She is jealous of anything outside her intimacy with Sergei. That includes people with whom Sergei spends a lot of time, Sergei's bachelor trips and excursions from which she is excluded, and family history which predates her and of which she is not a part.

Olga is by profession a scientist, and she has a deep mistrust of unverifiable theories such as Sergei's "threads." Despite her sincere desire to understand, and despite her unquestionable love for Sergei, she is unable to comprehend his point of view. Historical research seems simple to her, a matter of describing what already happened. She sees the past as a sequence of nations, epochs, and great men which the historian, like a policeman monitoring the line outside a movie premiere, merely has to keep in order. "Why," she wonders, "couldn't [Sergei] just sit diligently in the archives for a month—or two or three or five, as long as he had to—and pull out of that gigantic line everything that had to do with the Moscow Okhrana on the eve of the February Revolution, and then conscientiously work it all up into something presentable?" (AL 286).

Sergei's interpretation of the individual as the thread which transcends death, which connects the past "with the more distant past and with the future," flies in the face of Olga's vocation and disposition. For her, death is final. It is unambiguous; it destroys the molecular chain sustaining life; it leaves no loose ends, let alone loose threads. After Sergei's death, however, Olga is willy-nilly forced to recognize that chemistry is inadequate to explain what she is going through. Her science makes no provision for pain. It denies a physical basis for the grief that deprives her of sleep and overwhelms her with despair. "At first she thought that when all the threads, the most minuscule and delicate, were broken, she would find peace. But now it seemed that peace was unattainable, because the threads were infinite" (AL 261).

Sergei first assumes that the threads of history are embodied in individuals, descendants who are heirs to their ancestors intellectually or spiritually as well as physically. His "grave robbing" begins with his own forebears, who, like Grisha Rebrov's, include runaway serfs, religious dissenters, a defrocked priest, political deportees in Saratov, a teacher, and an idealist student in Petersburg. He sees an urge to dissent as a trait common to all of them, carried from one generation to the next and unextinguished despite the death of each individual. "The threads that extend out of the past, they are fraught [ves'ma chrevaty]. . . . Don't you see, they're fraught. . . . After all nothing breaks off without leaving a trace. . . . Final breaks don't exist, don't you understand? There has to be continuation, there must be, it's so obvious. . . . If one can keep digging deeper and further back, one should be able to trace the thread that leads forward" (AL 302–3). Hence he is eager to have tea with the grandson of a famous poet, to meet the old man who was once an Okhrana double agent.

But he is wrong. The grandson of the poet has no connection with his grandfather other than blood, and he talks more easily with Olga about housing than with Sergei about literature. The Okhrana agent has no memory left and can tell Sergei nothing. Even his existence does not constitute any proof, as Sergei had hoped, that the list of agents is authentic, since he remembers nothing. (No more is Irinka, Sergei and Olga's daughter, presented as being a form of immortality for her parents.)

It is Sergei himself who embodies the thread. His quest is sparked by the discovery that his father too was intrigued by double agents and had investigated the tsarist police and its use of informers. It is Sergei, not the Okhrana agent's grandson, who cares what happened to the old man once upon a time. It is Sergei's passion for the Russian past which provides the impetus for his research—into a subject Olga regards as a dead end and along lines that cause unpleasantness with Klimuk. Sergei is not frustrated by his topic or method; he is frustrated by the limitations placed upon them—the straitjacket into which he is forced to confine his work—and by his sense of isolation. His frustration leads him toward parapsychology, a last attempt to "trace the threads" that seem to elude him.

Parapsychology is shown to be a blind alley, neither hard science nor serious scholarship. Someone laughingly suggests to Sergei that he consult a clairvoyant: "That's what you should do, find a clairvoyant . . . and ask her about the anonymous informers! Maybe she'd reveal the secret" (AL 323). Shortly thereafter, Sergei abandons his dissertation (for a complicated mixture of reasons) and is drawn into this quasi-mystical pseudoscience, chiefly because the more conventional, more orthodox approaches are closed to him. Olga attends one séance, complete with table rapping. Trifonov emphasizes the foolishness, the deliberate self-delusions, of the people involved, much as Tolstoi does when Lydia Ivanova and Karenin consult Landau (the "mystic") on the question of divorce in *Anna Karenina*. Olga—like Stiva Oblonskii—listens with bewildered incredulity as the spirit of Herzen is "called up" and writes "through" the medium three words, one of them misspelled. Even Sergei, at some level deeply skeptical, lets out a snigger. But he sees no way out and he is desperate:

> And didn't he say that history was a magic mirror, in which you could see the future, and that he was ready to spend his whole life studying it. . . . He did say it, he did! And he did think so, he really did. But maybe something quite different was operating, a secret motive: to study so as to foretell. . . . Because it now seemed to him that all these infinitesimal details, these crumbs from the tables of some ancient banquets, which he fished up from the bottom of the well—nobody needed them save five or six people, nobody in the whole wide world. (AL 346)

Ironically, the woman who draws him most deeply into parapsychology, Daria Mamedovna, herself expresses contempt for the study of history—indeed, for all the humanistic disciplines. She pities that "scribbling fraternity" (*pishushchaia brat'ia*), all those who waste their time on superfluous nonsense. She is, in other words, no better than Sergei's institute colleagues, and she is much worse than Olga, who despite her discomfort and mistrust joins Sergei at the séance and even brings herself to ask Daria Mamedovna, of whom she is nearly sick with jealousy, to help Sergei find a way out of his deep unhappiness.

In the context of *Another Life*, continuity does not consist of individuals genetically linked. The "thread" is not a chemical chain of molecules. Such continuity as exists in life comes from interest, informed by love. It is given fictional formulation in the genre of "remembrance-contemplations," to which all of Trifonov's later work belongs. Just as in life the mere fact and exercise of memory are insufficient unless they are thoughtfully and creatively integrated and interpreted into the present, so in his fiction Trifonov demonstrates that it is not enough merely to refer to, recall, or recreate the past. It must be imaginatively considered and contemplated in the context of its consequence, the present. Otherwise it has no real meaning for that present. Otherwise it has no real meaning for the future. In the simpler fictions of the Moscow trilogy isolated flashbacks interpolate bits of personal history, and whispers of national history, into the dominating present. Such flashbacks serve primarily to recall times of greater innocence. Beginning with *Another Life*, past and present are melded as a way of presenting reality through the prism of time itself.

As Trifonov became more consciously certain that the past was integral to the present, he became bolder in his treatment of Soviet history. What are in the Moscow novellas only hints of the corrosively fearful Stalin years become, in *House on the Embankment* (*Dom na naberezhnoi*), a full-fledged examination of a Stalinist. His perturbation about the relationships between desirable goals and political expedience and between the degree of free choice and individual responsibility, on the one hand, and the sweep of historical momentum, on the other, took him from guarded and sidelong allusions to the years of revolution and civil war (even as late as *Another Life*) to a painful confrontation with the reality created by, as well as in spite of, admirable ideals.

Trifonov's work demonstrates his growing certainty that the ability to betray is closely linked with the willingness to forget, ignore, and distort the past. It is this theme that dominates both *House on the Embankment* and its successor, *The Old Man*. In *House on the Embankment* Trifonov returns to the times and themes of *Students*—to the anticosmopolitan campaign and to conformity and the price it exacted. He examines the mentality of one of the props of Stalinism, the "little men" on whom Stalinism depended and without whom that system could not have survived. In *The Old Man* Trifonov probes the roots of this system: the men and the ideas of Leninism, the choices made and the attitudes evinced throughout the revolution and Civil War which gave birth first to the monstrosity of Stalinism and then to the anomie so characteristic of modern Soviet society.

It Never Happened

One way of dealing with the past is by ignoring it. The protagonist of *House on the Embankment*, Vadim Glebov, attempts to do precisely that. In the modern Moscow of the first few chapters, Glebov is shown to be a privileged member of the Soviet elite, with a dacha in the country and permission to travel to Western countries. A chance meeting with an old friend, whom he at first barely recognizes, and their subsequent conversation on the telephone late that night, spark the journey into the past that constitutes the bulk of the novel. The action is set primarily in two epochs: the mid-1930s, culminating in the wave of terror which affected party members most acutely; and the late 1940s, culminating in the anticosmopolitan campaign. The central event of each period is an act of betrayal committed by Glebov and directly linked by Trifonov to Glebov's willful amnesia.

In the first instance the eleven-year-old Glebov is called upon to betray the names of boys involved in beating up the stepson of a high-level NKVD man, in return for help for his arrested uncle. He does so out of a mixture of motives which render him almost sympathetic. In part he is afraid that silence will harm his uncle Volodia, and in part he is desperate to get away before his rumbling stomach humiliates him with a loud belch. Naming two boys he dislikes, "he told himself this was quite fair, because those who would be punished were bad" (*HE* 231). Within a few days he manages to overcome the bad taste of betrayal by reassuring himself that nothing terrible happened to them.

This is Glebov's first betrayal. It is one conditioned by the atmosphere of the times, which Trifonov carefully delineates, not in order to exculpate Glebov but in order to portray the circumstances that influenced his actions. For Trifonov is depicting a symbiosis: Stalinism created men like Glebov and was in return sustained by men like Glebov. As Trifonov told an East German journalist in 1979, "Of course a man resembles his era. But at the same time he is to some degree—however insignificant his influence may appear—the creator of that era. It's a dual process."[19] A Soviet critic writing about the dramatization of *House on the Embankment* performed at Moscow's Taganka Theater echoed Trifonov's thought: "Every man is both a mirror of nature and a mirror of the flaws and merits of his age which . . . as it forms people, also forms itself by their actions."[20] In these statements both men are implicitly looking back to Herzen: "The individual is made by . . . events, but events are also made by individuals and bear their stamp upon them—there is perpetual interaction. . . . To be passive tools of forces independent of us . . . this is not for us; to be the blind instruments of fate—the scourge, the executioner of God, one needs naïve faith, the simplicity of ignorance, wild fanaticism, a pure, uncontaminated, childlike quality of thought."[21]

Some of the Bolsheviks in *The Old Man* demonstrate precisely such faith, simplicity, and fanaticism. Glebov never does. Trifonov shows us rather his fear of embarrassing himself, which is both recognizable and forgivable. He also shows us a self-serving kind of calculation that implies moral cowardice, which is much harder to forgive. Glebov himself, we learn, was one of the ringleaders of the attack on the boy, though, typically, he stood aside and let others do the actual fighting. He has been raised in the shadow—literal and metaphoric—of the looming house on the embankment. He is envious and resentful of the power he imputes to its occupants. He is surrounded by a miasma of fear in which sensible adults avoid any kind of conspicuous behavior. So the eleven-year-old Vadka Glebov has already internalized the value of advantageous connections and the logic of taking the easiest way out of a tricky situation.

Glebov's culpability in betraying his friends is mitigated in part by his youth and in part by the fact that he is being used by his vulnerable parents in ways he doesn't understand, for as a child he is still somewhat innocent. Our own negative assessment of Glebov's behavior derives less from the denunciation than from his self-exoneration: "When Glebov feels that he had behaved correctly and 'said the truth about bad people,' and when 'the sense of having betrayed someone' bothers him only for a few days we begin to distance ourselves."[22] Moreover, as we later learn from the first-person narrator, something terrible *does* happen from the point of view of the betrayed boys: one of them ends up having to leave his home.

Glebov is no longer a child at the time of his second betrayal, in the spring of 1948. The air is rank with slogans: "petty bourgeois tendencies," "excessive admiration for foreign scholars," "toadyism" (*nizkopoklonstvo*). The campaign gets under way at Glebov's institute with attacks on one instructor for knowing only "literary" language, not the alleged "language of the people." In the battles of the anticosmopolitan campaign, politics and ideas are not the real issues: power is. Despite the veneer of ideological jargon, principle is patently less important than vengeance, however thinly veiled. Power is shifting from those who were in the ascendancy immediately after the war to a new group, their erstwhile subordinates.

This time Glebov betrays Professor Ganchuk, a man who is at once his dissertation adviser, his mentor, and his future father-in-law. When Glebov is called into the director's office he does what he did as a child: he takes what seems to be the easiest way out, agreeing to apply for another supervisor for his dissertation. He thus accedes to his own involvement. Trifonov ironically paraphrases Glebov's thoughts: "If only he had known where it would all lead! But in some things Glebov was a little slow-witted, lacking in foresight." Glebov has many qualities, but dullness and lack of calculation are not among them.

In his attempts to wriggle out of the anti-Ganchuk campaign, Glebov does not understand—*chooses* not to understand—that once the decision to get rid of Ganchuk is made, the "grounds" and the "proof" will be found. His inquisitors are trained to sniff out the particulars of any heterodoxy: hidden Freudianism, camouflaged Menshevism, inattentiveness to class struggle.[23] Glebov can be under no illusion, except one he wills himself to believe, that the matter is unimportant. It may in truth be idiotic and trivial, but in reality it is serious and fateful for Ganchuk. Since at some level Glebov understands this full well, he then attempts to convince himself that Ganchuk, like the "bad boys" twelve years earlier, deserves what is going to happen. There is no real difference, he wants to think, between the way Ganchuk behaved, without "hesitation or pity," when he was a member of the Cheka and the way his adversaries are behaving now. There is no difference between Ganchuk's calumny of former opponents and the calumny now directed at him, other than the fact that Ganchuk's days of ruthlessness and cruelty are over.

Does it matter that Ganchuk and his revolutionary peers acted in the name of ideals in which they sincerely believed, while the current crop of vigilantes are impelled by careerism, ambition, or fear? Does sincerity matter if the result is, in both cases, that innocent people suffer? In a late story, "Short Stay in a Torture Chamber," Trifonov speaks bitterly of sincerity. He describes how he was hounded during the anticosmopolitan campaign and rehearses the bitter words he will address to his chief denouncer fifteen years after the event: "You behaved sincerely. There is nothing nobler and more remarkable than sincerity! . . . You didn't think about what your sincerity would turn into. . . . Your sincerity is wickedness!"[24]

At issue, however, is not Ganchuk's behavior in the 1920s. At issue is his victimization in 1949. Ivanova notes that "Ganchuk is far from being a positive hero for Trifonov. But his opponents . . . are poison."[25] Glebov puzzles over the relative decency of Ganchuk versus Druziaev and Shireiko for a long time, thereby evading his own moral dilemma. He is not being asked to judge, to the best of his ability, the validity of a specific grievance, let alone Ganchuk's overall merits or flaws. He is being asked to participate in a kangaroo court. And he knows it: he considers the attack on Ganchuk a "sickening business." Yet he manages to reassure himself with a combination of self-deceit and evasion. A fellowship is the reward for his testimony; he pretends he wants it less for the money than for the "moral boost" it represents. He pretends not to understand that failing to act is quite as meaningful, and has consequences as real, as taking action. His bitterest complaint is not that he has been asked to inform on Ganchuk but that he has been told to do so at a meeting where others can hear him and will condemn him: "They didn't mean, 'Say your piece'—they meant 'smear yourself with shit.' Come to the meeting and pour shit over yourself in public'' (*HE* 485).

Trifonov makes sure to show that Glebov has backed himself into a corner. There are genuine alternatives to his behavior. A range of characters similar in age and status to Glebov react in a variety of ways, from completely corrupt cynicism to valorous (and, in the circumstances, possibly self-destructive) loyalty. Trifonov allows Glebov to consider the alternatives in a narrative passage that mimics Glebov's thought processes. Reading it, we understand both *what* he thinks and *how* he thinks. Because Glebov knows that Ganchuk is fundamentally different from those who are out to destroy him, he must find an argument to justify his own betrayal. What he comes up with is that nothing he can do will matter anyway: to try to save Ganchuk would be a form of suicide, like "swimming against a current that carries everything before it" (*HE* 487).

It is a familiar argument, albeit one degraded from its original Hegelian context of history inexorably on the march. It offers reassurance to many of Trifonov's characters—Glebov, surely, but much better men than Glebov as well. Metaphor obscures the real dilemma they face: history becomes a flood, "the times" become a flow of lava, an airstream, a current. Such images, with their connotations of overwhelming force and concomitant human helplessness, comfort the individuals who use them. Yet although there may be some truth to them, Trifonov insists that they are first and foremost excuses, alibis for weakness (in Berlin's phrase), and unacceptable. The world Trifonov portrays is dramatic, fissiparous, and concerned with defining itself. It lacks a sense of fatalism and the concept of misfortune. His characters, even when they experience blows of fate, consider themselves tested or on trial; they believe they have choices.[26] And so they do. When Glebov makes his choice, he fails his test.

Glebov learns to live with the choice he has made in what Primo Levi calls "the transition from falsehood to self-deception":

More numerous [than conscious liars] are those who weigh anchor, move off, momentarily or forever, from genuine memories, and fabricate for themselves a convenient reality. The past is a burden to them; they feel repugnance for things done or suffered and tend to replace

them with others. . . . The distinction between true and false progres-
sively loses its contours . . . [and a man] accustomed to lying in public,
ends by lying in private, too. . . . To keep good and bad faith distinct
costs a lot: it requires a decent sincerity or truthfulness with oneself; it
demands a continuous intellectual and moral effort.[27]

Glebov is not capable of such an effort. He tries hard to forget his
fight with Ganchuk's main defender eight years after the event,
when his guilt and fury at being reproached explode in violence.
He tries to forget the frozen white face of Ganchuk's wife; she has
been fired and dies soon thereafter. Most of all he tries to forget
his betrayal of Ganchuk's daughter, the entirely innocent, wholly
victimized Sonia. His credo is, "Whatever one doesn't remember
ceases to exist." But as the meeting that opens *House on the Embankment* reveals, that is not quite true. Glebov prospers at the cost
of rejecting his own past, which means rejecting what was good or
potentially good in him. It is not so simply done. An Indian residing
in Africa in one of V. S. Naipaul's novels recognizes this: "It isn't
easy to turn your back on the past. It isn't something you can decide
to do just like that. It is something you have to arm yourself for, or
grief will ambush and destroy you."[28]

III

Old Men

The *Old Man* (*Starik*) continues and amplifies many of the themes central to *House on the Embankment*, but there are salient differences. In some ways *House on the Embankment* is the bolder work within the Soviet context. By depicting the kind of man who abetted the abuses of Stalinism, the transformation of his psychology, and the material success engendered by that transformation in a society by implication equally transformed, *House on the Embankment* anatomizes a state of mind and an era that were virtually taboo in official Soviet literature until years after Trifonov's death. *The Old Man*, in contrast, merely alludes to the Stalinist years; instead, Trifonov turns to the years of revolution and civil war. That choice makes *The Old Man* more radical than *House on the Embankment* because it implicitly connects the Stalinist period with the years (and actions) that preceded it and challenges some of the most sacrosanct assumptions about the Bolshevik period. *House on the Embankment* is narrow in focus. In it Trifonov examines the personal cost of forgetting for one individual, Vadim Glebov. The angle of vision for *The Old Man* is wider, encompassing what happens to a whole society that forgets or deliberately distorts its past.

In *The Old Man*, as in all of Trifonov's works, modern Soviet society is portrayed as lacking ideals and idealism. The Moscow creative and technical *intelligenty* who populate Trifonov's fiction are isolated and lonely. The symptoms of this malaise are evident as much as ten years earlier, in the Moscow trilogy; in *House on the Embankment* and *The Old Man* the causes are made plain. One critic has argued that Trifonov, in search of a more moral life than the ruined present, found it not in the actual past but in an idealized version of the past.[1] Certainly his sympathies are nearly always with members of the older generation, in part because the older generation is more likely and more willing than the younger generation to remember. Forgetting the past and ignoring history or rewriting it for a variety of reasons are shown as the root causes of modern Soviet discontent and accidie.

Those reasons need not always be venal or self-serving. In *The Old Man* Trifonov carefully demonstrates how emotions—jealousy, love, envy, resentment—color and distort even the most honorably intended exercises of memory. But deliberate distortion is a matter of choice. The subtext is well understood by Trifonov's attentive readers: were the Stalinists heirs of the Leninists or traitors to them? Did the behavior and decisions of the Stalinists in the 1930s and 1940s stem from the policies and actions of the Bolsheviks during the revolution and civil war, or did they violate those policies and actions?

Of Tsars and Revolutionaries

The centrality of history is emphasized from the first page of *The Old Man*, with the letter the hero receives from his childhood friend Asia Igumnova. In elliptical phrases which the reader does not yet understand, Asia alludes to the key historical moments out of which *The Old Man* is constructed: the years of their childhood and adolescence in Petersburg before the revolution; the Civil War and its cruel division of families and friends into opposing sides; terror both White and Red; the trial of Sergei Kirillovich Migulin; the post-Stalin rehabilitation of individuals.[2]

Hard on the heels of the letter, the old man of the title, Pavel Evgrafovich Letunov, joins his family on the veranda of their dacha where they are in the middle of a heated debate on the role of Ivan the Terrible in Russian history. Letunov, despite his absorption in the study of the past, dismisses the debate as no more than a personal feud between his son and son-in-law. Ironically, the man obsessed with the relationship of ends and means is unable to see the point of "arguing about tsars." Yet this is hardly just an argument about tsars. It involves the meaning of Russia's history and the nature of its national character, and as such it is part of an old debate, in which "sides," or categories, tend to become identified with individuals (Ivan the Terrible, Peter the Great) and movements (the Jacobins, Slavophilism). In an analysis of the contemporary version of the debate, Alexander Yanov delineates the alternating "Brezhnevist" and "Stalinist" phases of authoritarianism that constitute Russian history. The "Stalinist" phases, rigid and convulsive, cannot survive the death of the particular tyrant, and "times of troubles" ensue—the name given first to the chaotic, anarchic dozen years between the end of the Rurik dynasty and the enthroning of the Romanovs at the turn of the seventeenth century. The freedom, or anarchy, of those interregna engender "soft" and stable "Brezhnevist" periods, which fail to reconcile the rigidity of the "Stalinist" phase and the flexibility of the interstice, thus producing a new restoration of Stalinism.[3]

In *The Old Man* battle is joined on three issues. Pavel Evgrafovich's son-in-law, Nikolai Erastovich, defends Ivan the Terrible on grounds of historical context, political expediency, and national interest. First, he says, the times were bloody everywhere in Europe, and Ivan was no worse than other monarchs of that period. Second, the goal of expanding the Russian empire justified the warfare necessary to achieve it. Finally, Ivan was a great patriot; he "did everything and more for Russia" (*beskonechno mnogo*; *OM* 12). Nikolai Erastovich's last defense exudes more than a whiff of Russian nationalism, an intimation later reinforced in a discussion about his religious faith.

Letunov's son, Ruska, his outrage fueled by an all-day drinking spree, refutes Nikolai Erastovich point by point. Historical context is double-edged, he shouts: the sixteenth century may have been a time of carnage but it was also the time of the Renaissance and Michelangelo. The new territories weren't worth gaining at the cost of so much bloodshed. And far from benefiting Russia, Ivan the Terrible's true legacy was the division of Russia's population into butchers and victims, a total corruption of the nation.[4] The parallel with Stalin is unmistakable, and it is made even more pointed when Ruska mentions Ivan's flight during the Tatar invasion; the reader cannot help but think of Stalin's bizarre behavior after the Nazi attack on June 22, 1941.

Thus from the very outset *The Old Man* shows itself to be a novel built on the past, out of what are, broadly speaking, the two central experiences of Soviet history: Bolshevism and Stalinism. Yet the wish to remember and understand the past, a concern whose primacy Trifonov insists on both for its own sake and for the sake of understanding and creating a desirable present, is by no means a central concern of all the characters, neither in the present nor even in the somewhat idealized past. During the Civil War, Letunov's Bolshevik colleagues in the Don region feel a blood tie with the past. They see themselves as part of history, referring often to the French Revolution and their spiritual paradigms, Danton and Deputy Julien. They find "inspiration, legitimacy . . . and a usable vocabulary of politics" in the French Revolution: "Revolutionaries, precisely because they are creating something new (or something that they think is new) look to history as a source of corroboration for their efforts that their ideas, as yet untested, cannot provide. History becomes for them a form of metaphor, an analogy in the past for what will happen in the future."[5] Yet the Bolsheviks' highly selective knowledge of history is confined almost entirely to examples of "justified" terror. Shigontsev, a Bolshevik who sat in the tsarist labor camps together with Letunov's uncle Shura, "bursts with quotations and examples from the French Revolution," chiefly to justify ruthless policies toward recalcitrant Cossacks. He and the even more ruthless Braslavskii cite Deputy Julien: milk is good nourishment for children, but blood is the food for the children of freedom. Braslavskii knows so little of history that he likens himself, a representative of the Red Army, to Carthage—a *force* of destruction instead of its victim. "I'll march like Carthage through this village!" he declares (*Po etomu khutoru ia proidu Karfagenom*). Sadly, it is his ignorance rather than the pride he takes in his destructive power which astonishes Letunov.[6]

The Cossack schoolteacher Slaboserdov attempts to explain to these Bolsheviks why—given Cossack history and traditions—the Bolshevik policy toward the Cossacks is so wrongheaded. He is brusquely interrupted: "We don't have time to listen to history lectures. . . . Later, perhaps, when we have time to kill after the victory of World Revolution." Slaboserdov firmly—if vainly—protests: "But it is historical questions that you are deciding. So it wouldn't be a bad thing for you to take a look at history" (OM 80). He wants to warn them that the Cossacks will revolt if forced to give up their saddles, their harnesses, their weapons. And so they do. But of all the Bolsheviks listening to him, only Letunov's uncle Shura recognizes the force of his argument, and Shura, on the brink of a serious illness, is overruled.

In the present of the novel—that is, in Moscow and the dacha colony in 1973—very few of the characters take much interest in the past. Letunov's daughter, Vera, is childless and unhappy; she has her hands full dealing with her cranky husband and has neither energy nor interest to spare for her father's quest. Ruska shares some of his father's values, including a remnant of the kind of idealism that motivated Letunov fifty years earlier. Thanks to that vestigial idealism Ruska volunteers to fight peat fires in the burning summer of 1973. But he too is unhappy, drinks too much, and loses his job. The present is a far more pressing concern to him than a long-gone past. Ruska's kindly son, who questions his grandfather about Denikin and the Civil War, does so out of love for Letunov and to please him, not because he especially wants to know the answers.

The most openly contemptuous attitude is represented by—indeed incarnated in—the character Kandaurov, the "iron boy" familiar to Trifonov readers from virtually every one of his works. He is the prototypical pragmatist whose definition of *good* is whatever serves his interests, and he lives by the precept of doing everything "to the limit" (*do upora*). Kandaurov lives exclusively in the present. We know nothing about his background or family both because he is self-creating and because as soon as the present becomes the past he discards it.

Kandaurov is not a monster. In some ways he is even likable. He is far from stupid, and he is shrewd enough to know when and how to use influence, money, curses, threats, or flattery to get what he wants. Only rarely does he miscalculate, because he assumes that other people are like himself, and he is not wrong very often. He is insensitive and he lies as a matter of course, not merely to avoid unpleasantness but because he doesn't believe there is such a thing as objective truth. As a pure relativist, he believes only in expediency. Truth, like good, is a function of circumstance. Thus when Svetlana, his mistress, says at their last meeting, "I envy women men don't lie to," he replies: "There are no such women." Kandaurov does not actually commit a vile act. "But," one critic correctly observes, "the power of artistic persuasion is such that the potential for such vile acts is perfectly obvious to us, as is all of Kandaurov's respectable baseness."[7]

Because of his all-too-successful attempts to live exclusively in an unanchored present, Kandaurov is a moral cripple living a death-in-life similar to Glebov's in *House on the Embankment*. Ironically, just as he is about to achieve his greatest successes he is dismissed from the novel, struck down by the fate that he always believed he could direct and the chance that he always assumed he could manipulate. (Routine medical tests required for a coveted assignment in Mexico turn up a serious malady.) Since he has jettisoned his past and is abruptly deprived of a future, his present becomes irrelevant and he disappears; we know of him at the end only obliquely, through the image of his suffering wife.

Of all those who "forget," Kandaurov is the most extreme, for he is willing to obliterate the past entirely, and his motives are wholly venal. His mother-in-law, Polina, distorts her own past. In order to get into an old-age home for Civil War veterans, she claims to have been a "revolutionary activist" when she was only fourteen years old. Letunov is both shocked and amused by her deception, but when he repeats to his grandson Polina's version of her past, he exaggerates for the sake of a better story and to hold Viktor's interest. There is nothing terrible or corrupt in this; it is natural, commonplace. But it shows how the past can become distorted even by those who are most concerned with representing it accurately and truthfully.

Others forget because it hurts too much to remember. The most poignant example is Sanka Izvarin. As a child, Izvarin lived in the dacha colony and had a German governess. His father vanished in 1937 or 1938; he and his mother were pushed out of the colony, and his mother died in the winter of 1938. For decades Izvarin has repressed the devastating memories of 1937–38; he remembers only when he actually sees an old neighbor, whose big nose triggers a memory of his mother's intense dislike of the man. Then "the memories came of their own accord," somehow all the fresher for having been avoided for so long, like clothes packed away in a cedar chest. Izvarin does not choose to forget out of disdain for the past. His forgetting is one way of dealing with—if not ever coming to terms with—the trauma of abandonment, of sudden orphanhood, of fatherlessness, which recurs in every one of Trifonov's late works. It is a carapace meant to protect him from reliving the pain.

Yet "memory is an unreliable thing," Pavel Evgrafovich thinks to himself as he rereads Asia's letter and compares it with stenographic records of Migulin's trial. In *The Old Man* it is generally emotion that makes memory unreliable: Asia's love for Migulin, Letunov's love for Asia. While both recognize the force of their feelings, neither is able or willing to understand how those feelings influence what they recall of the past.

Asia, like nearly all the women characters in *The Old Man*, is essentially apolitical. (Letunov's mother, a committed revolutionary in her own right, is the only exception.) Such political loyalties as the women have derive from their men. Asia's mother would happily damn all politics in 1919 if she could only have her family back together, alive and united. Letunov's wife, Galia, once ostracized their neighbor Prikhodko, not because as a onetime Kadet (Constitutional Democrat) he was politically "unreliable" but because she suspected him of having hurt her husband. Asia reacts the same way, viewing the entire Civil War in the Don region, both at the time and in retrospect, through the prism of her love for Migulin. She senses who is "for" Migulin and who is "against" him.

This perception of truth is intuitive: Trifonov emphasizes its dissociation from reason and intellect by using the verb *chuiat'* (to sniff out). It is also presented as a uniquely "female" quality. As such it echoes the nineteenth-century tradition of Dostoevskii and Turgenev. (Tolstoi, by contrast, did not assign this ability solely to women; all his children have it, and so do a few wise male characters like Kitty's father, old Prince Shcherbatskii, in *Anna Karenina*.) In *The Old Man* it is a faculty even minor women characters possess. Kandaurov's young mistress, for instance, senses that her lover is lying to her; Letunov's daughter-in-law senses that Ruska has another woman. When Letunov resents Asia's division of people into categories of "us" and "them" based on their attitude toward Migulin, what he really resents is that she perceives him as an enemy— and that she is right.

Asia's love for Migulin was stronger than her deep affection for her cousin and first husband, Volodia, stronger than her love for her third husband, Nesterenko. It transformed her from a joyful girl into a wary adult. When she writes to Letunov, trying to reconstruct the past as she remembers it, she interrupts her narration of the events of 1919: "I'm not defending him, Pavel. I just cry, weep, when

I remember how he came running to me, cursing someone. . . . I just loved him and was awfully sorry for him" (*OM* 197).

Like Izvarin, Asia has spent many years trying to repress events that were highly charged and painful, as well as dangerous to recall until Migulin's rehabilitation. The memories triggered by Letunov's questions are permeated with her love and fear for Migulin. She tries to recall facts, but what she recalls most vividly are emotions: his vacillations, his sense of suffocation, his despair when his arrest is ordered, his contempt for a petty and vindictive regimental commander. She forgets details of their three-week campaign en route to the front line and the identity of various individuals because those are far less important than her emotional memories. When, finally, Letunov travels to Asia's town "to find out the truth" about Migulin's treason, Asia has no more answers for him. She has exhausted her memory's store of information and factual truth: "I wrote everything that I could. I don't know anything more. . . . I never loved anyone in my long, wearisome life as I loved him" (*OM* 255). Like Keats in "Ode on a Grecian Urn," Trifonov sets up a tension between different kinds of truth: factual truth that may be found in documents and transcripts, undistorted by time and memory; and emotional truth that resides in feelings and perceptions. Keats's urn finally speaks

> because the speaker has ceased to ask it those historical and extrapolatory questions which it is not equipped to answer. The urn is only a "silent form" when the wrong kinds of truth are asked of it. As soon as Keats sees it as a friend of man . . . it speaks, and becomes an oracular form, saying . . . two things equally true. It says "Beauty is Truth" when we are looking at it with the eyes of sensation, seeing its beautiful forms as actual people, alive and active. It says "Truth is Beauty" when we are looking at it with the eyes of thought, seeing it, as the mind must see it, as a marble inscribed by intentionality, the true made beautiful by form. The two messages do not coincide; they alternate.[8]

The Mask of Ideology

Ideology plays no role in the present time of *The Old Man*. Neither token adherence nor even hypocritical obeisance is paid by a single contemporary character to Marxism, Leninism, Bolshevism, or any other -ism. For the people who populate Moscow and its environs in 1973, ideology is entirely irrelevant. In the Civil War sections of *The Old Man* ideological dedication is pervasive, yet it often masks, consciously or unconsciously, emotion; passions masquerade as principle. *The Old Man* encourages the reader to infer that this disappearance of ideological framework may be rooted in its misapplication and abuse in the past.

The most egregious example is connected with Bychin, who was in February 1919 *revkom* (revolutionary committee) chairman of the Mikhailinskaia *stanitsa*, a large Cossack village. Bychin is a kind of latter-day Nechaev.

> A consideration of Nechaev's career poses clearly for the first time a vital question that the twentieth century has been forced to live out, if not to resolve: the question of revolutionary ethics. What are the sources of value and what are the moral limits, if any, for a secular revolutionary confronting the established order? . . . Nechaev believed that *the revolution itself conferred all value.* Neither his revolutionary contemporaries nor his revolutionary successors have been able to accept him. Nor have they been able to repudiate him.[9]

(In 1914, as a schoolboy, Letunov heard revolutionary "morality" invoked to justify biology laboratory experiments: "Great ends require victims!" "But the victims disagree!")

It is a time and place of intense fighting. Among the forty or so people Bychin arrests as suspected counterrevolutionaries are the two sons of the schoolteacher Slaboserdov. Only later do we learn that behind Bychin's ideological vigilance lies personal hatred. He wants the sons executed not, in fact, because of any harm they might cause to the revolution but for vengeance. Friends of the Slaboserdov family—but not the two boys—had badly beaten Bychin's brother for "rumpling up the teacher's daughter in the garden" (*uchitelevu dochku v sadu pomial*; *OM* 77). It is not clear if this was an act of rape, as it sounds, or—as Bychin claims—an act of love, his brother's revenge for being rejected as a suitor by the family. It *is* clear, however, that Bychin's real motives in wishing to get rid of the Slaboserdovs have much more to do with envy and resentment than with any real or imagined political disputes.[10]

Ideology screens emotion in the Migulin affair as well. The party's suspicions of Migulin, while to a degree explained by his disagreements with Bolshevik policies, have more to do with psychology than with politics. They are rooted in mistrust of his obstinate independence and his Cossack loyalties. He is not like the majority of the Bolsheviks, especially the leadership. The emotional factors that shaped perceptions of Migulin, and judgments of his behavior vis-à-vis the Bolshevik high command in 1919 and 1920, are still evident in both Asia's and Letunov's re-creation of those events.

Letunov claims he needs to know why Migulin disregarded orders and set off for the front in August 1919. In fact, however, he seems to answer that question quite satisfactorily. Migulin was driven nearly mad by the mistrust he felt on the part of the Bolshevik leadership. A proven military leader, he could not bear the immobility to which his orders confined him, and he was determined to help defeat the Whites. Migulin admitted at his trial that his actions were treasonous insofar as they directly contravened orders, but he justified himself in terms of his lifelong search for justice and his deep concern for his people, the Cossacks. Both impulses led him to find the system (and party) that promised the most equitable division of goods and land. In the end he threw in his lot with the Bolsheviks, to whose cause he was genuinely (but not blindly) committed.

The sequence of events, as reconstructed from the documents Letunov has amassed along with his own recollections and Asia's, makes all this reasonably clear. It follows, then, that Letunov needs answers to other questions, at once broader and more personal. He wants first of all to understand himself. Deeply involved in the Migulin affair as secretary of the 1919 tribunal, he has a need to understand his own role in it. According to Ivanova, "Letunov is convinced that he is investigating the Migulin case, but really he is sorting out the Letunov case."[11] Second, his children and grandchildren have inherited the Russia that was born then, born as much in Balashova near the Don as in Petrograd or Moscow, as much at Migulin's trial as in the storming of the Winter Palace, as much in Trotskii's articles about Migulin in *Pravda* as in Lenin's April Theses. When, years earlier, Letunov was explaining a detail of the events of 1919 to his wife, he implied as much: "The truth which was created in those days, in which we believe so ardently, has inevitably lived on to this day, has become reflected and refracted, has become the light and air which people don't notice or guess at" (*OM* 185).

For those people, then, Letunov wants to set the record straight. He believes that "a people can face the future only when they have fully and imaginatively lived their past," and he wants to bequeath to his children a heritage of truth.[12] Pavel Evgrafovich is as conscious of the distortions produced by time and memory as his creator is of the additional legacy of officially sanctioned distortions. He is less aware of the "schizoid activity" of writing history:

> It involves imposing upon the past, but also stripping away from it, layers of retrospective interpretation. It aims to reconstruct "what actually happened," but it goes about this in apparently contradictory ways: by allowing preoccupations of the present to determine what we find relevant from the past, so that history becomes a device for explaining how we got to where we are; but also by rejecting such "presentism" on grounds that those who made history can hardly have had our concerns uppermost in their minds when they did so. To say that the past affects the present but that the present affects only our perception of the past is to point out an obvious asymmetry.[13]

Professional deformation apart, Letunov's unselfish motives are unavoidably mixed up with his own emotions, his own fears and dreams. Even he, honest though he tries to be, cannot admit the extent to which his memory of Migulin and the trial is colored by his emotions, especially by his old, unrequited love for Asia, which began when they were children. In 1919 Letunov both envied and was jealous of Migulin. He resented Migulin's offhand condescension, which emphasized his own youth and unimportance, and he feared Migulin as a wedge between himself and Asia. He could not repress a fierce joy upon hearing of Migulin's arrest, and he was uncharacteristically brutal when Asia, frantic with fear, offered herself to him if only he would help Migulin: "Forever? Or just for today?" he had asked her. "That was a terrible question," he remembers with shame, "base and not like me! I couldn't have asked that if I'd been myself!" (*OM* 221).

His refusal to give full weight to his love for Asia on a conscious level shifts the conflict into his subconscious, where it takes expression in two nightmares. In one, Letunov conflates Asia and his late wife, Galia. Galia is terrified, but not for him; she cries, but not for him; she loves someone boundlessly, but not him. In his second nightmare Letunov sees a man and a woman embracing, recognizes them as Asia and Migulin, and kills Migulin with a blow on the head. But even these transparent messages do not overcome Letunov's deep reluctance to admit how, and how much, his emotions cloud his reason.

Neither does Letunov recognize that his love for Asia provides an impetus unique to him, different from the elemental forces he *does* admit and with which he tries to exonerate or at least justify himself. Fifty years after the fact, Asia's rejection—her eternal love for someone else, never for him—still gnaws at him, influencing his memory to an extent that he persists in hiding from himself. Objective circumstances may have "proved" Migulin's treason; the "lava" of history may have blinded the Bolsheviks. As Letunov told Asia at the time of the trial, "Denikin is advancing, they've taken Kursk, a plot's been discovered in Moscow, a bomb went off in Leontev Alley, our comrades have been killed. . . . In this hour of mortal danger, how do you expect a man to be judged when he admits to treason?" (OM 221). Nevertheless, it is apparent that Pavel Evgrafovich believed in Migulin's guilt not, fundamentally, because of the circumstances or the lava, or, for that matter, because of Migulin's self-incrimination. He believed in it primarily because of Asia. He condemned Migulin in the hope that with Migulin gone he would somehow manage to win Asia's love—at long last—for himself.

Indeed, the article he has published rehabilitating Migulin and his continuing research are attempts to cleanse himself of his guilt and make reparations for the role he played in the past.[14] In remembering those times, Letunov offers two versions of the past that deliver essentially incompatible messages. One version relies heavily on linguistic devices to convey the elemental, anonymous forces that were at work during the Civil War years. The critic Igor Dedkov points to the prevalence of impersonal verbs (*smylo, uneslo, utopilo, otrezalos' navsegda, proneslos' mimo, issokhlo, ischakhlo*: wiped away, carried off, buried/drowned, cut off forever, passed by, dried up, wasted away) in the portions of the novel dealing with the past.[15] He and others note the frequency with which the past is compared to the elements: tremulous air, flood, froth of blood, volcanic lava, currents of hot and cold wind that sweep individuals along and away. In such a flood-washed world, man is merely a cork tossed about on the waves.

Yet such metaphors gloss over the responsibility each individual bears and for which he can be held accountable. Dedkov drily remarks that from Letunov's description of why Migulin died—the collision, in a fateful time, of two streams of warmth and cold, of belief and unbelief—one might think no people were involved, that Migulin's death was as inexorable (and unpredictable) as an act of God.

Ivanova points out that Letunov skips over not just his part in the Migulin trial but two other betrayals as well: he mentions 1928 and then corrects himself by substituting 1935, thus implying that both years involved betrayal. "Letunov's paradox is the paradox of self-deceit, a form of salvation required for existence but which doesn't suffice for one's conscience. . . . He was 'weak' more than once, three times he denied his conscience." Trifonov debunks the idea of a passive, blind subordination to the lava; he does not accept the capitulation of the individual, although he does recognize the force of events: "On the one hand the 'arrow' of history could be slightly deflected in its path; on the other the historical process is not infinitely variegated, but singular. On the individual depend both an understanding of the direction of that process and responsible participation in it."[16] We are back in the realm of Herzen: "Our paths are not unalterable at all. On the contrary, they change with circumstances, with understanding, with personal energy. The individual is made by . . . events, but events are also made by individuals and bear their stamp upon them—there is perpetual interaction."[17]

Trifonov counters the "elemental forces" of Letunov's memory in two ways. The simpler is a counterexample, the character of Letunov's admirable uncle Shura. Shura is able to withstand "the flood." He remains unswervingly devoted to his cause, yet he is able to consider and assess other points of view objectively. Shura is the closest thing to a positive hero in *The Old Man*. Although he is at times powerless to prevent Bolshevik errors or temper Bolshevik brutality, he at least recognizes those errors and that brutality and attempts to avert them. Thus his inability to prevent the murder of Slaboserdov's sons is ameliorated, if not excused, by his being delirious, with a high fever, when they are shot. He leaves town rather than participate in what he knows will be a phony trial of Migulin. Shura's departure, though it leaves him with clean hands and unblemished integrity, is something of an evasion and a tacit admission of failure on Trifonov's part: when Shura cannot change a course of events he knows to be wrong, Trifonov preserves his heroic image by getting him off the scene.

Shura is not blinded by the lava, but he is only one man. In order to demonstrate the fallacy, or at best evasion, of holding elemental forces responsible for human decisions, Trifonov offers a second version of the past.[18] This is the past Letunov constructs and reconstructs out of documents he finds in archives and dusty file boxes, "old bits of paper" which reveal that specific decisions were made by specific individuals who must bear responsibility for them.

Remembrance-Contemplations

In the first part of *The Old Man* there are virtually no documents. Letunov recounts his memories of the years in Petersburg before and during the revolution, and of events in the Don region, by paraphrasing and summarizing speeches, telegrams, and conversations. In the second half of the novel many of those same incidents are presented via texts. The reader thus has two views of the same episodes. The Bolshevik directives against the Cossacks are a case in point. First they are presented as Letunov recalls them: he was not permitted to read the text of the directive at the time, and he saw it only some fifty years later. His memory minimizes their horror both by picking out trivial details and by using metaphor: "It's ludicrous, the stupidities that were committed: stripes down your trouser-legs were forbidden, you couldn't use the term 'Cossack,' they even abolished the word '*stanitsa*,' you had to call it a '*volost*.' As if it was a matter of words and stripes! They thought they'd plane down a people in three months. My God, how much timber was felled that spring!" (OM 76).

The directives are far more than a matter of "words" and "stripes." They mandate mass terror against Cossack leaders, grain confiscation, destruction of any food surplus, forcible relocation to the Don region of peasants (i.e., non-Cossacks) who would be equal in status to Cossacks, the disarming of Cossacks and the arming of non-Cossacks, and so on.

What Trifonov copied into *The Old Man* is still not the text verbatim. Letunov's paraphrase of the text is less extreme than the directive itself: it modifies or abridges some of the worst clauses. Herman Ermolaev, who compares the text of the directive with the text given in the novel, notes omissions which minimize both Lenin's role in approving the policy and the extent of the terror. The most material modification changes the clause *"Provesti bezposhchadnyi massovyi terror po otnosheniiu ko vsem kazakam, prinimavshim kakoe-libo priamoe ili kosvennoe uchastie v bor'be s Sovetskoi vlast'iu"* (Carry out merciless mass terror against all Cossacks who took direct or indirect part in the struggle against Soviet power) to, in *The Old Man*, *". . . presledovanie vsekh, kto imel kakoe-libo otnoshenie k bor'be s sovetskoi vlast'iu"* (the prosecution of anyone who had anything to do with the fight against Soviet power). Trifonov's version does not fundamentally alter the meaning, but the substitution of *"presledovanie"* for *"bezposhchadnyi massovyi terror"* certainly softens the phrase.[19]

The documents in the second half of *The Old Man* suggest the extent to which ideological considerations blinded most of those involved to common sense and pragmatism, not to mention traditional morality. Their inclusion conveys the tension of the struggle of that "'ferocious year' . . . [giving rise] to the conclusion—which emerges as if by itself—that truth and faith are inextricably woven."[20] When Migulin and Shura send a telegram to southern front headquarters in an attempt to convey an accurate picture of just how bad Cossack morale is, they are ignored. A few days later Migulin sends another telegram to Moscow to impress on the Bolshevik high command the impoverishment of its Don resources. He minces no words: misjudgment can cost the Bolsheviks victory. He asks for social development that people can see and participate in (*stroitel'stvo glasnoe sotsial'noi zhizni*). He heaps scorn on the available troops and gives a realistic assessment of what role his corps can play against Denikin's regrouped forces. He describes the mood in Cossack villages as so hostile to the Bolsheviks that many Cossacks are advocating the reinstatement of the tsar. Such gloomy candor merely increases the Bolsheviks' mistrust, as we see from the comment Trotskii scribbled on one of Migulin's telegrams: "Don Cossack Establishmentarianism and Left Social Revolutionaryism."

The documents cumulatively reveal the responsibility borne by individuals for specific decisions. Migulin blames "pseudo-Communists" for actions damaging to the revolution. He blames especially "all the scoundrels who have artificially roused the people as a pretext for eliminating them." His reading of the situation seems accurate. But Letunov makes excuses out of a reluctance to admit that virtually no one wanted to hear what Migulin was telling them. Migulin's letter, he says, was read by "other people" than those who should have read it, and those who needed to read it didn't see it in time. There were no "real commissars," like Furmanov and Chapaev, who would have properly assessed Migulin's warnings; and Lenin, who "understood the essence of the [Cossack] problem," didn't know the details of this particular case. (Ermolaev, noting that Trifonov presents Trotskii as the main source of mistrust, comments: "There is not a word in the novel about the fact that Lenin, in August 1919, attached 'enormous significance' to the apprehension of Mironov, who had set out against Denikin.")[21] Letunov keeps sliding away from the point.

It is not the facts that are at issue during the trial. Migulin pleads guilty to the bulk of the charges. The truth, however, is something more than the facts alone. The documents—the directive of the Revolutionary Council declaring Migulin an outlaw and traitor; the indictment; excerpts from Trotskii's piece on Migulin and from the trial transcript; Migulin's exchanges with the president of the court; the testimony of several witnesses; the closing statements of prosecutor, defense attorney, and defendant—prove to be as unreliable in their own way as the fallible memories of individuals. They do not distort the past the way that memory does. Unlike the modifications time works in all human memory, the texts are fixed, inscribed, and unaltered. But they reflect the biases, preconceptions, and needs—political, emotional, and psychological—of the people involved no less than Asia's love influences her memories and Letunov's jealousy of Migulin influences his.[22] Trotskii's article, for instance, purports to state a fact: Migulin was an exploitative careerist. Yet the article appears two days before the start of the trial, and, as Shura says with vehemence, only the trial can establish such "facts."

Facts are hard enough to establish. As one old man, annoyed at Letunov's version of Migulin, retorts, "There are no facts!" Letu-

nov's very first attempt to produce the "facts" of Migulin's life exemplifies the problem: *"the facts* are the following: Migulin is now
46. *If* he is a revolutionary, he's really one of the old ones. *But they*
say he's still a powerhouse, strong on the march and good at horse
racing and wood-hewing. . . . *Everyone claims* that there's more—that
he's educated, that you can't find a better-read, more literate man"
(*OM* 72; emphasis mine). In four sentences supposedly relaying information, there is actually only one fact: Migulin's age. His cred-
ibility as a revolutionary is moot, and the remaining attributes are
hearsay. Migulin's very war record is uncertain: Letunov mentions
his decorations, adding, "even the Saint George's Cross, I think."
His uncertainty does not impugn Migulin's bravery, but it under-
scores Letunov's lack of information and his reliance on other
sources, an ironic initiation into the unaswerability of certain
questions.

As a young man, almost a boy, Letunov was satisfied with facts.
As an old man seeking an answer that encompasses the psyche and
the heart as well as the mind, he comes to better appreciate that
the correlation between fact and truth is only approximate, that the
two cannot be equated. The truth of the Migulin affair must take
into account more than facts. It requires cognizance of the poisonous atmosphere that surrounded—and choked—Migulin, and his
acute frustration as an active military leader who was forced into
passivity. It must recognize his fear that the revolution was being
undermined and might even be destroyed by scoundrels. It must
understand his philosophy, not inaccurately characterized by the
prosecutor Yanson as "semi-Tolstoyan," "semisentimental," and
amateurish. It must acknowledge his masculine pride, which impels
him to show off to Asia, and even his vanity, which is insulted by
the order to stay put.

Trifonov, disinclined as ever to pronounce direct comment on
the ethical and political issues involved, by no means avoids judgment. He conveys his views through linguistic devices, narrative
voice, and structural montage. In this case a brief scene abruptly
implodes the present into what has been a steady re-creation of the
past. Letunov is writing a reply to Asia's letter when he hears shots.
Women and children are shouting and crying because a group of
men are shooting the dogs in the dacha colony—supposedly on
orders from the dacha trust—and tossing the corpses into a truck.

Prikhodko, Letunov's old enemy, claims that it is a matter of "orders," but Letunov realizes that behind Prikhodko's reliance on orders lies personal spite. Letunov is especially horrified that one of his grandsons has been infected by the frenzy, joining the butchers and shouting, "Let's shoot Arapka!" (the family dog). But Letunov protects Arapka, and he is joined by a few children who put their arms around the dog to safeguard him.[23]

This menacing 1973 scene is preceded by Asia's letter and the indictment and followed by the trial transcript. Trifonov thus links past and present. They differ in one salient respect: no principles are at stake in 1973, merely callousness and greed. The modern murderers, unlike those half a century earlier, can be bought off with a three-ruble note. But Letunov's grandson, a modern variant of his own young self in Balashova, is blinded by mob fever no less than he himself was blinded by the lava. The scene, especially the alliance between the weak (the aged and the young) against the strong, conveys the notion that individuals can indeed resist the lava, can take a stand and influence, perhaps change, the course of events. They can protect and defend those more vulnerable and defenseless than themselves, defeating even armed representatives of authority who supposedly speak for the collective. By including the incident with the dog butchers, Trifonov passes judgment on those who manipulated the Migulin trial, and on Letunov himself, with his protestations of helplessness and repeated references to "the course of events" and the "icy voice" of the revolution.

Letunov considers it his mission to learn the truth by piecing it together out of the shards of the past. "Writing the truth of what happened in history," notes David Malouf, "is a matter of taking the records and then listening hard between the lines for the cries of individual agony and protests. It demands the highest imagination."[24] Letunov explains his motives to a couple of psychiatrists:

No, my dear doctor. I feel guilty not toward *him* [Migulin], but toward all the rest, including you—yes, guilty. . . . Guilty of not having shared the truth. Of having stashed it away for myself. And it seems to me, my dear Candidate of Medical Sciences, that the truth is precious only when it is for everyone. If you keep it for yourself, under a pillow like Shylock and his gold, then the hell with it, it's not worth spit. That's why I'm torturing myself in my old age, because there's no time left. (OM 251)

His need to understand, and to share that understanding and expiate his guilt for having kept the truth to himself, keeps him up all night poring over old documents. It propels him to Asia's apartment. It is that need which makes him admirable, despite his betrayals and compromises. Implied throughout *The Old Man* is the notion that the Bolsheviks' distortion of the past, while it may have been understandable, went hand in hand with moral abdication. Their exploitation of history for their own ends provided the underpinnings for the grosser and more calamitous abuse of historical truth and moral decency that occurred during the Stalin years.

Strategies

IV

Pressures

As a Soviet citizen and the child of "makers of history," Trifonov was concerned with the truth of his country's past because of its affect on his own life and on the contemporary society it had generated. As a Soviet novelist, Trifonov was preoccupied with the rewriting of history because he worked under the perpetual onus of censorship during his thirty-year career. Certainly in its final decade, and marginally before that, his work staked out territory new to Soviet literature. It did so in a repressive atmosphere in which the parameters of what writers could hope to publish were continually, if unevenly, shrinking. Yet Trifonov was consistently able to publish what he wrote, by and large in the version that he wrote. Because of his access to official channels of publication he was occasionally disdained by those outside the system as a writer who settled for half-truths.[1] One need not share that view to acknowledge the likelihood that Trifonov had internalized the demands imposed by Soviet literary censorship.

Two kinds of censorship affect the work of a Soviet writer. Internal, or self-censorship, is patently a complex, elusive, and private process. Absent a psychotherapeutic relationship with the author, a reader can only trace the spoor of such a process in language, imagery, and patterns of ellipses. External censorship, by contrast, can be more easily analyzed—if not precisely quantified—for a given period. For the post-Khrushchev period, with its fluctuations in the degree and nature of political pressure, information about Soviet procedures is available; we can even compare the strictures applying to belles lettres with those operating on scientific or historical publications.[2]

Thus editions of the same text dating from different years can be compared to elicit clues to the differing demands imposed by the censors at different times. By carefully examining the 1963 and 1979 editions of *Slaking the Thirst*, for instance, Tatiana Patera demonstrates that what Trifonov once dubbed "arguments about the times" often prove to be a function of the times themselves. The 1963 text contains references to the Twentieth Party Congress and to Khrushchev's boldness and his condemnation of Stalin's errors. In 1979 those references were simply deleted. A line in the earlier edition pertaining to an arrest in April 1937 was dropped, as was a description of a character trying to find out about the fate of a prisoner.[3] In a comparison of three texts of "Pigeon Death" (1968, 1971, and 1978), Patera finds a similar pattern of deletions: in 1971, allusions to the 1956 amnesty of prisoners and to the anti-Semitism of the early 1950s were cut, as was the description of an arrest. It is plausible to conclude, with Patera, that such cuts were the result of a hardened political climate.

Yet withal, there is often no definitive explanation for the appearance of a controversial work. Decisions of censors and editors can be so arbitrary that even extremely knowledgeable people can offer no more than conjecture. The publishing history of *House on the Embankment* is instructive in this regard. When *House on the Embankment* appeared in 1976, its anomalous status was swiftly recognized: the issue of *Druzhba narodov* containing *House* sold out at kiosks almost instantly and was available only on the book black market for grossly inflated prices;[4] it was removed from library stacks in "at least two suburban towns."[5]

Speculation was intense: how, people wondered, was Trifonov able to publish a work that exposed the moral cowardice of those who actively or passively abetted the Stalinists? One rumor circulating at the time gave credit to Sergei Baruzdin, editor of *Druzhba narodov*; supposedly he was very ill and didn't care about the consequences. Certainly Trifonov had Baruzdin's protection. Moreover, since *Druzhba narodov* was generally regarded as a conservative journal, it perhaps received less scrutiny from Glavlit (the censorship office) than more "liberal" magazines like *Novyi mir*.[6] An émigré who claimed to have been on the staff of *Druzhba narodov* at that time later explained the publication of *House on the Embankment* as a fluke; it was a substitute for a more controversial manuscript about the construction of the Moscow Metro which the censors blocked at the last minute.[7] It may also be possible that the censor liked *House*, perhaps because he could see himself in the character of Glebov, whose moral cowardice is depicted with what can be construed as some degree of compassion.[8] External circumstances also helped: the emigration and/or expulsion of what was by 1976 a substantial number of the most prominent artistic figures of the Soviet cultural world increased pressure on the authorities to keep those whom they could. Trifonov, who had never been an open dissident, was a likely candidate.

The chain of censorship is complex. *House on the Embankment* slipped through the net of prior censorship for its initial publication, but once published it triggered a vociferous and at times vicious reaction from the literary establishment, led by *Literaturnaia gazeta*. The novella was branded "ideological subversion" at a special session of the Writers' Union held in April 1976, and its publication in book form was nearly blocked. Trifonov had to fight for even the small edition that finally appeared: a print run of 30,000 instead of the more usual 100,000.[9]

Whatever the explanation for the censors' approval of *House on the Embankment*, its publication—without any changes imposed by them—liberated Trifonov, freeing him to write *The Old Man* in a very short time. Had *House on the Embankment* been severely cut, he might well have given up his investigation into Soviet history as a professional dead end.[10] Neither *The Old Man* nor *Time and Place*, which Trifonov prepared for publication and which appeared within months of his death, was censored to any significant degree.[11] The story cycle known as *The Overturned House*, also published several months after Trifonov died, was basically uncensored as well, with the major qualification that of its seven stories, only six appeared in print initially. The seventh was published years later, as was the novella *The Disappearance*.

Neither the omitted story nor the novella could be printed during the Brezhnev years. They are—for Trifonov—unusually explicit treatments of politically sensitive subjects. *The Disappearance* contains a description of an NKVD search and Trifonov's re-creation of the mephitic atmosphere of 1937–38. It details the psychological effect of the Great Terror on Old Bolsheviks like his father, who engaged in denial almost until the moment of their own arrests. The story, "Short Stay in a Torture Chamber," recalls the 1949 meeting at which Trifonov was expelled from the Komsomol for having lied about his father's political status ("enemy of the people") as well as for his general anti-Soviet behavior.

Both *The Disappearance* and "Short Stay in a Torture Chamber" became acceptable in the radically different publishing climate initiated by Mikhail Gorbachev, as did a few minor texts. Apart from *The Disappearance* and "Short Stay," the only other posthumous publications of significance are segments of Trifonov's memoirs about Tvardovskii that were excluded from the previously published text.[12] The censored portions deal chiefly with the brutal treatment meted out to Tvardovskii in 1969 and 1970, before his magazine was taken away from him. Trifonov also matter-of-factly describes Tvardovskii's alcoholism; an open secret among the Moscow intelligentsia, Tvardovskii's addiction had been kept from the public in a conspiracy of discretion.

Not surprisingly, Soviet writers in the past rarely wrote about the effects of either externally imposed censorship or self-censorship. Until recently, émigrés were the main source of information and analysis about the constraints to which they were formerly subjected. They all agree that self-censorship is part of virtually every Soviet writer who functions within the system.[13] Anyone knowledgeable about the functioning of the Soviet literary establishment must assume that Trifonov paid a price for his long and generally successful career, though he rarely participated in the shameful public obeisances made by the Writers' Union to the party and was one of only seven courageous members of the Moscow Writers' Union to object to the expulsion of Solzhenitsyn in 1969. Similarly, anyone conversant with the realities of Soviet literature, even a fervid admirer of Trifonov's work, must assume that he made compromises in his work.

Inferentially, from the published texts, and directly, from conversations with both Soviet and émigré writers, one is persuaded that certain gifted writers who wished to explore politically sensitive themes found or devised artistic means to circumvent and thwart those constraints. Trifonov was one of them. The trademarks of his prose style—an obliqueness of approach, a tendency toward ellipsis, multiple narrators, and symbolic freighting of the details of ordinary life—were enforced by censorship conditions. They may even have begun as a conscious obfuscation of the censors. Eventually, however, they came to signify his deep belief in the unseen but real connections between events, individuals, and historical eras.

Political necessity proved artistically fertile. As Trifonov matured as a writer and expanded the areas his work explored, he developed more complex strategies for expressing his thoughts. To articulate the political orthodoxy and categorical judgments of *Students*, the novel which won him a Stalin Prize in 1950, the twenty-five-year-old Trifonov had little need (and perhaps little command) of metaphor and symbol, structural montage, or interplay of narrative voice. The nexus of choice, fate, and circumstance that forms and informs moral decisions in his works twenty years later, however, is far more subtle. Delineating that nexus required of Trifonov a language and a style artistically persuasive and accessible to the reader for whom he was writing. He expected attention and alertness from that reader, his "partner," and he both revoked and rewarded such attention with a complex manipulation of aesthetic devices.

V

Narration

Two aspects of narrative technique consistently served as Trifonov's primary means of at once evading censorship constraints and conveying his increasingly complex understanding and judgment. One is narrative structure, the other is narrative voice. In earlier works set mostly in the present, and even in the Moscow novellas, Trifonov employed flashback or retrospective narration to intensify the connection between past and present. As the past swims into a character's consciousness by association with the present, the events of many years and a character's personality development can be compressed into a small space.[1] In the fiction of the 1970s such juxtaposition of past and present within a character's mind became a means of demonstrating the interrelationship among different kinds of times, not merely different time periods.

Structural Montage

Like memory, art does not operate in linear fashion as it seeks out time's traces; it is discontinuous, it gets lost, it takes detours. Thus Trifonov's use of flashback and foreknowledge is not merely a matter of style but an expression of his concept of time as a force which is not stable or measurable and which can go backward and forward.[2] As such, it almost parodies the conventionalized Soviet vision of time as hierarchical, with a radiant future casting its glow on present-day pallor and a shadow hanging over even the radiant,

heroic (Leninist) past.[3] In his final work, *The Overturned House*, an-
titheses of times and places become the very building blocks of the
stories, contrasting principles bridged by the *I* who narrates them.

In the internal monologues the first-person voice affords Trifonov a direct means of plunging into the past. Thus Pavel Evgrafovich Letunov, the hero of *The Old Man*, continuously shifts
mentally between the present world of his Moscow dacha in the
1970s and the years between about 1912 and 1920. His thoughts
resurrect past eras; presented as a stream of associations, they demonstrate the relationship between historical time and personal, individual time. The text shifts, often with no transition at all, from
an omniscient narrator who seems to be peering over Letunov's
shoulder to Letunov himself. Partly in mimicry of the vagaries of
memory, his first-person voice moves freely from 1919, when his
best friend Volodia was killed by the Whites, to 1920, when he
preached Marxist theory to a bitter woman whose family was destroyed by the Civil War. The year 1914, when he and Volodia were
students together in Petersburg, gives way to the heady days of
March 1917 and the furious speechifying of 1921. Letunov's first-
person voice propels us into the past, as does Trifonov's use of
present-tense verbs for the episodes set in the past—a time more
real and much more meaningful to Letunov than the present. In
The Old Man Trifonov creates a mood of turbulence out of the
literary equivalent of cinematic hard cuts, using short phrases that
have the effect of stage directions: "Dark nights, wind, pitch black-
ness, frost. Enter Slaboserdov the teacher."

The symbiosis of historical time and personal time was crucial to
Trifonov, both philosophically and aesthetically. Even in *Time and
Place*, where historic events are shifted to the side and the decisive
moments occur in the wings or backstage,[4] particular details of individual lives refer and allude to events of national, sometimes international, significance. The revolution and Civil War are absent
from *Time and Place*, except via the fragmentary recollections of an
elderly woman who experienced underground life during the tsarist
years. The major events of Soviet life in the middle third of this
century—the purges, the war, the anticosmopolitan campaign,
Khrushchev's secret speech, the ensuing amnesty of political prisoners—are presented in shallow focus, as limned backdrops to the
full-color, sharply delineated events of the characters' lives occu-

pying the foreground. Yet historical design and meaning pervade the trivial, everyday details; because of that immanent meaning they are raised to the level of symbol, sign, and pictogram.[5] Every detail does double duty: as the quotidian manifestation of contemporary life, and as a sign of the flow of historical time.[6] Tropes, figures of speech, and connectives are missing from the novel, strengthening the sense of urgency and the pressure of time.[7]

Time and Place begins with precisely the sort of indirect depiction of historical events that characterizes the novel as a whole. Eleven-year-old Sasha Antipov and his friends are swimming in the Moscow River, fooling around and pushing one another under. They laugh, choking on water; they call back and forth, "spies, spies, little spies" (shpiony, shpiony, shpionchiki), the last word of which delights them with its rhyme, ponchiki (donuts). The device of putting the taunting, destructive language of Stalinist accusations in the mouths of children who do not understand what they are saying enhances the effect of the words. Precisely such a crooked mirror is used to intensify the horror of the children's "game" in Aleksandr Askoldov's 1968 film Commissar (released in 1988), in which very young children catch and tie up their terrified sister, all the while giggling and calling out in piping voices the insults they have heard without comprehension, such as "filthy Jew."

As the children warm themselves in the sun on the far bank of the river, they describe what they have seen at the dacha colony in recent days: papers being burned and people leaving suddenly and unexpectedly. They do not understand what they are describing. The scene conjured up is one of total innocence, a childhood idyll over which hangs the threat that will take away Sasha's father and destroy the boys' innocence forever.

Even at the moment of their lightheartedness, "reality"—the reality of a given historical time—intrudes. Back on the beach the father of one boy is furious that his son was pushed under by the others. He grabs Sasha's ear, twisting it as if Sasha were an adult who had committed an act of sabotage, not a child playing with friends. Forcing him to the ground, he refuses to let go until Sasha gives up. He is not simply mean or intemperate; he is a mean, intemperate man whom the times have empowered, indeed licensed, to indulge himself at others' expense.

The child Sasha initiates a pattern of response that will be characteristic of him as an adult whenever pressure is exerted on him: stolid silence. He does not explain; he does not run away. Sasha's mother intervenes, but to Sasha's surprise, although she addresses his tormentor with contempt, she evinces neither empathy for his pain nor admiration for his stoicism. She is in a hurry to go back to Moscow, and we understand her unusually cool and unmaternal behavior as another sign of the door slammed shut on Sasha's childhood. Overlaying the scene is what Ivanova calls the "particular tension between the wholly ordinary occurrence and the simultaneous fateful event . . . like the ambiguity of a word used both in its literal and metaphoric sense."[8]

The same effect is created in *The Disappearance*, when Trifonov overlays the adult world of 1937 with the child's world, creating a kind of transparency for the reader. For the eleven-year-old protagonist, Gorik, the year 1937 marks the one hundredth anniversary of Pushkin's death. That centennial celebration of Russia's greatest literary genius preoccupies Gorik's whole family; everyone helps him collect Pushkiniana for his school contest. If for later generations 1937 has become inextricably associated with the Moscow Trials and the purges, Trifonov shows us that the child's 1937 was filled with the Spanish Civil War and the Pushkin jubilee. (The coincidence of timing is terribly ironic: the murder of Russia's intellectual elite at the hands of the state occurring simultaneously with homage to Russia's greatest poet.) Not even the Pushkin centennial is immune to the Terror. One of the best exhibits, a collage of Pushkin's head made with real (poodle) hair, doesn't win a prize because the boy who made it "suddenly moved out of his house and no longer went to the school. The next day the head was removed from the exhibit and thrown out somewhere." It is the sense of innocence victimized which makes the removal of the Pushkin head from the school exhibit so painful.

The two "times"—personal (in this case, child's) time and historic (adult's) time—are always shown in coexistence; our perception of their interrelationship requires this confluence. At one point Gorik, intent on swiping his uncle's flashlight for a planned cave trip, listens absently as the adults talk about "all kinds of stuff"— Spain, politics, the Hittites, enemies of the people, Shmidt's polar exploration, Karl Radek, and Feuchtwanger. Normalcy prevails: his uncle is contrary "as ever," his father argues with his grandmother "as usual." Gorik's mother, home from a business trip, is pleased that there is hot water for her bath; her brother describes Ordzhonikidze's greetings to his factory, which will be printed up in a brochure. The atmosphere of predictable, habitual family life is real. Given the public reality, however, it is also carefully constructed, appearing whole but ripping apart like rotted fabric at the news Gorik's father brings home: Ordzhonikidze is dead, an apparent suicide.

In both *The Disappearance* and *Time and Place*, the loss of a father is presented not in what is said but in what is unsaid. At the end of *The Disappearance* Gorik's father assures him that they will again be in the stands watching the New Year's parade through Red Square next year, but Gorik intuitively knows that they won't. The private experiences of Gorik and of Sasha Antipov, whose father broke his promise to return in time to take *him* to a parade, acquire the depth of a generational experience both by what the reader knows to have happened and by the text itself. Trifonov suggests the ephemerality of not merely Gorik's and Antipov's age of innocence but of a national innocence that evanesces like "the trace of an airplane in the blue skies."

Fifteen years after Sasha Antipov's father disappeared, Sasha's wife, Tania, is pregnant with their second child. Again, the shadowy presence of large historical events anchors the complex interdependence between "public" history and private choices in the novel. Antipov and Tania have resolved on an abortion (at that time still illegal) because their life is so unstable that they fear for the future of a new child. There is a faint implication in the text that in such parlous times nothing can be excluded: they might disappear, they might be arrested.

The abortion is scheduled for what turns out to be the day of Stalin's funeral. The doctor is delayed because of the funeral. There are no taxis, the streets are impassably thronged with people, and the atmosphere is of a heavy and nearly palpable dread. Tania's distress and fear of the pain are mirrored in her aunt's anxiety lest the neighbors in the communal apartment inform on them. At the same time, Stalin's death engenders nebulous, uncircumscribed fear and uncertainty. Alluded to in abstract language, the event is less like a human death than an elemental shift in the axes of the universe. People's faces are "mournful, meaningful, even ceremonial" (*torzhestvennyi*). Antipov hears sobs: the neighbors are mourning Stalin in the kitchen.

Trifonov juxtaposes Tania and Antipov's suffering—given poignant intimacy by the water put on to boil and the doctor's casual, affectionate language—and the grand, state-level suffering caused by the national trauma of Stalin's death. What connects the two is the fear that Antipov senses, in the room and on the street, in the steamy air of the kitchen and in the icy air outside. Despite their pervasive fear of the unknown, at the last moment Antipov and Tania decide against the abortion. They take a chance on the new life the baby symbolizes and which may be in store for the country as a whole. Thus Trifonov tries to show the connection between the fate that creates the choices for an individual who fortuitously occupies a certain place at a certain time and the responsibility an individual bears for the choices he makes.[9]

The structure of most of Trifonov's novels is dramatic. They are built around a moment of crisis in the hero's moral condition; a prehistory to that crisis is alluded to, but we meet the hero when he must make a choice. In *The Exchange*, for instance, the hero is introduced and presented almost exclusively in the context of his mother's illness and the moral dilemma confronting him as a result of it. In *Taking Stock* the hero's mental recapitulation and evaluation of his life is spurred by discovering his son's degraded and immoral behavior. In *House on the Embankment* the protagonist is presented in essentially two vises of moral choice—during his childhood, and when he is in graduate school during the late 1940s.

Time and Place is unusual for its epic form; Ivanova calls it a "*zhizneopisanie*" (life study) and likens it to a *zhitie*, a medieval Russian saint's life, a genre that formulaically follows a rigid sequence of events in the life described, including childhood, testing, martyrdom, and beatitude.[10] This is the only work in which Trifonov traces the life of his hero in conventional stages, beginning with childhood, moving through the stages of adolescence, first love, apprenticeship, professional success, moral crisis, near death, and ending with a wholly human rebirth involving a new marriage and a new child.

Essentially, however, it does not matter if moral choice is compressed into one or two critical moments or expands into a lifetime of experiences, because that lifetime comprises choices. Each chapter of *Time and Place* focuses on a crisis involving a character, usually Antipov, in some sort of moral dilemma. The possible consequences of the choice vary, but each time something important is at stake. If Antipov accedes to expedient editorial "suggestions" in 1947, his story will appear in print—but it will not be "his" story anymore. If he names the man who illegally appropriates tobacco during the war, that man will be arrested. If he and Tania go through with the illegal abortion in 1953, they will have no second child. In *Time and Place*, no less than in Trifonov's more typically structured works, the self is repeatedly and existentially defined the same way, from myriad decisions and actions.

Obviously, Antipov's decisions do not affect him alone. What he chooses to do has an impact on the fate of other people. Yet Trifonov consciously deprives individuals of the aura of extraordinary drama, even though their behavior creates a moral chain of effects.[11] In his attempts to evade resolving those dilemmas Sasha resembles Trifonov's other protagonists: Dmitriev, Glebov, and Letunov. Eventually, despite their distaste, these men do what is asked of them. Sasha Antipov also chafes at pressure and seeks avenues of escape, and some critics have suggested that Trifonov concentrates on Antipov's vacillations and weakness rather than on the choices he ultimately makes.[12] In the end, however, he invariably makes the "honorable," the "right" choice. Antipov tries very hard not to be merely "a cork on the flow of time, tossed about by it"; he tries to understand his place in that flow and to follow his own path.[13]

Voices

The first-person voice fulfills several roles in Trifonov's late works. As noted above, it often effects the shift from present into past in the hero's mind. It allows Trifonov to manipulate reader sympathy as well as to express his own judgment. It combines with the characters' voices to create a generational experience. For that generation, the central experience it narrates is the loss of one's father, a deprivation afflicting at least one character in each of Trifonov's late works.

Orphanhood, specifically loss of father (*bezottsovshchina*), is a condition found in an extraordinary number of works by Soviet artists

of Trifonov's generation: Vasilii Aksenov's *The Burn*, Anatolii Rybakov's *Children of the Arbat*, Tengiz Abuladze's film *Repentance*, and
Anatolii Pristavkin's *A Golden Cloud Passed the Night* are but a few.
For those born between 1925 and 1937, the dread, impersonal, and
destructive might of history (revolution, civil war, and world war)
was compounded by the particular depredations of Stalinism. The
scope and dimensions of orphanhood transcend the limits of personal tragedy and suggest an entire society bereft of its fathers.

Today, sadly, younger generations of Soviet artists portray a society again—or still—populated by homeless, parentless children.
The circumstances are different, but the result is much the same.
In the films of Dinara Asanova, especially the 1983 *Kids* (*Patsany*),
in Roland Bykov's 1984 film *Scarecrow*,[14] in Liudmila Petrushevskaia's plays and stories, in Vladimir Makanin's novellas, and in Iurii
Nesterov's poetry,[15] children are raised by grandparents or aunts,
by drunken, abusive fathers or weary mothers. Often, turfed out
into an unaccommodating system, they are not raised by anyone
at all.

In the case of those who lost their fathers in the Stalin years,
circumstances until recently barred writers from addressing directly
this central, fundamental trauma. In a literary world constricted by
censorship, Trifonov was not able to examine causes and assign responsibility explicitly. What he could do was exploit the opportunities of his medium, in particular the opportunity provided by
narrative voice. As he probed the Soviet past, particularly the events
that impinged on his own life, Trifonov gave a character in each of
his later books his own experience of the disappearance of home
and parent. That character, speaking in the first-person voice, articulates the sense of loss felt by the child whose safe world vanishes.
He is not the hero, though he is usually acquainted with the hero.
He is an observer of the action rather than a participant in it. While
he is not the author, he speaks for the author in this particular
context, expressing his pain and the pain of his compatriots.

The Fatherless I

At the end of *Time and Place* the first-person narrator muses on the
difficulties between fathers and children. His grown daughter is

afraid of "losing" her father; the son of the novel's protagonist, his own alter ego, Sasha Antipov, has "lost" his father to a new wife. They have not really lost their fathers, however; they have lost the old relationships they had with their fathers—the child's sense of being the center of his parent's world. They have lost the security of being able to take their fathers' love for granted, without having to stake a claim. That loss is painful, but it is an inevitable and necessary step in growing up. The narrator dryly comments, "In my childhood there were also problems with one's father, but different ones." His generation lost their fathers to unnatural violence and mystery, to a conspiracy of lies. They never had the chance to mature into an adult relationship, a rough kind of equality.

The *I* thinks to himself that fathers "cannot be lost," a statement true in a metaphoric sense as long as memory functions. But it is not emotionally true. For Trifonov, as a Swiss critic has noted, conjuring up and re-creating a past time delivers him from the overwhelming force (*der Gewalt*) of history which deprived him of his father; it creates a kind of immortality.[16] All the "versions" Trifonov gives of this deprivation share certain key elements. The basic facts are always the same: the father goes away (often "on business"), fails to come home, and thereby breaks a promise to his son. The child receives no explanation from his mother, who herself soon disappears. The family dacha and/or apartment must be vacated; the child must move far away. The emotions felt by the boy are also consistent in each repetition. He is angry at his father's "betrayal." He is bewildered and confused that his mother, previously a reliable source of love and comfort, neither defends nor helps him. He feels ashamed and guilty, as if somehow he is to blame. He hates leaving his known, safe world, his friends, his courtyard. And he has a foreboding that nothing will ever be the same again.

Thus it happens, for example, in *House on the Embankment*, to the unnamed *I* who played with a group of children that included the novella's protagonist, Glebov. In the third of the four episodes he narrates, this *I* describes the eviction of himself, his sister, and his grandmother from the house on the embankment to a room in a communal apartment somewhere on the outer edge of Moscow. It is a scene of desolation: the boy is leaving behind the locale of his whole life, his best friend Anton, and most of all the girl he loves, Sonia Ganchuk. He does not say, but the time and circumstances inform the reader that his parents have disappeared in the purges. (The only open reference in the novel to the purges of 1937–38 occurs in relation to Glebov's uncle Volodya.) The pain the *I* feels at being torn from his previous life is mixed with obscure shame: the family must have done something wrong or they wouldn't be forced to move. His shame is confirmed by the elevator man's flick of condescension toward the family: by moving out, it ceases to exist. The *I*'s suffering may be childish, as he himself says with the perspective of hindsight, but it is genuine.

In *The Old Man* Trifonov gives the core story of his autobiography to Sanka Izvarin. Middle-aged when he is forced to recall the events of 1937–38, he—like his counterpart in *House on the Embankment*—reacts with the pain of the bruised child he was. Like Trifonov, Izvarin spent childhood summers and holidays in a dacha colony which he was forced to leave after his father's disappearance. His mother died the winter of 1938. (For the twelve-year-old child that Trifonov then was, the arrest of his mother must have seemed a deprivation almost as sudden, total, and mysterious as death.)

The memories of those events, long repressed, surge into Izvarin's consciousness with force and freshness at the sight of his erstwhile neighbor, Prikhodko. Izvarin remembers the "dirty trick" Prikhodko had "played" on him and his family: the childish language reflects the integrity of the memory, preserved intact like a fly in amber. Prikhodko, a grown man, had accused the child Sanka of breaking another boy's leg on purpose. Sanka recalls Prikhodko's words: "The father sabotaged the job he was on and the son is doing the same thing in his own circle, crippling other children." The recollection is horribly painful. It brings back a world that did not evolve naturally into a new phase of his life but was destroyed.

Once Sanka Izvarin begins to remember, national history and personal history are inextricably intertwined. His governess, Maria Adolfovna, left after his father's arrest because his mother could no longer afford to pay her. Dread—it is, after all, 1938—so infected this kindly and affectionate woman that she was afraid to visit or contact the family. Despite her caution she was deported in 1941.

Izvarin recalls the Burmin family, who advocated "progressive nudity" with the fanaticism of ideologues. ("The bourgeois," said

Burmin, "hide their filthy souls beneath their hypocritical clothes.")
Izvarin's father was contemptuous of Burmin, but during the Terror
it was Izvarin's father who was arrested, while Burmin was "swept
up onto the crest of a wave of monstrous force." Izvarin remembers
his last birthday party at the dacha, shadowed by their imminent
eviction. The world he had known and grown up with disappeared
forever from the earth that year, "crumbled and collapsed like a
sandy bank," and yet what is buried under the collapsed bank still
exists, in his memory. Memory, in Dmitri Likhachev's words, "is the
overcoming of time, the overcoming of death."[17] Izvarin recognizes
as much, thinking that "nothing existed independently . . . nothing
ever disappeared completely."

In *Time and Place* there are so many orphans that the *I* becomes
their spokesman, *primus inter pares.* The first chapter narrated by the
I portrays the loneliness of three orphaned children: the narrator
and his chess partner Levka, who are both about twelve in 1937–
38, and Levka's country cousin Minka, a few years older. The *I* lives
with his grandmother because his parents are "on a business trip"
(*na komandirovke*), a grotesque euphemism in those years for their
actual location. Levka has no father; his mother, Agniia, lives with
the mentally ill Stas. Agniia, a nurturing woman by nature as well
as a nurse by profession, brings Minka to Moscow after she "loses"
both her parents. Minka is so alone that she envies the *I* because
he at least has a grandmother. This is a blighted world, a world of
what Trifonov calls "alien grief and unneeded goodness." The fragile and artificial home Agniia attempts to create for her manufactured family ends in shards, victim of more violence.

The *I* in its purest state is used to tell this story, whose consistency is unique in Trifonov's literary universe. Insisting that the past
is knowable, Trifonov at the same time insists on its complexity.
Hence almost every event is told from several perspectives and from
many points of view. His intellectual resistance to the determinism
of Marxist analysis results, artistically, in rejecting the certitude of
a single omniscient narrator.

But the loss of a parent is a singular experience. It is repeated
obsessively in book after book, but within that pattern of repetition
it is singularly told. Once activated, Izvarin's memory is the only
version of the events he describes: we are not given Prikhodko's
view or that of Ruska Letunov, the boy whose leg was broken. In

Time and Place we are given the child's view of what happened: his father promised to return in time for a parade, but he failed to return in time for that or anything else. We understand much more, from which our sense of the tragedy of the scene derives. But the child is simply confused and angry. This is what he knows: his father broke his word. In other words, while Trifonov usually offers multiple points of view on any particular event, in order to show both its complexity and the distortions imposed by individual memories, he repeatedly presents that central trauma through what amounts to his own twelve-year-old eyes. It seems that there *is*, there can be, no other version of that event, no other "reality," than the one he perceived.

The I as Judge

The first-person voice further serves Trifonov as an indirect means of judgment. Soviet writers have traditionally been expected to yea their yeas and nay their nays loudly and unambiguously. Throughout his career Trifonov was accused of "over-objectivity," an allegation that could be quite damning.[18] Critical norms demanded the clear enunciation of authorial position. "Only through authorial position, through the author's evaluation of what is being portrayed," wrote one typical critic in the mid-1970s, "can the responsible social tendency [*grazhdanskaia napravlennost'*] of a work of art, its moral and social significance, appear."[19]

When *House on the Embankment* appeared, Trifonov was criticized for his supposed neutrality toward Glebov, for merely "showing that life without drawing any conclusions."[20] (On the other hand, he was charged with implicitly condemning the comfortable life led by high officials, who "deserved" their comforts.)[21] Doctrinaire critics were dismayed by the absence of explicit praise and condemnation; nondoctrinaire critics, both Soviet and Western, were confused, conflating Trifonov's voice with those of his characters.[22]

This "neutrality" is deceptive. In fact, Trifonov unfailingly renders judgment on the behavior and choices of his characters, and he reveals that judgment in large part by his manipulation of the first-person narrator. Especially in conjunction with other narrative personae, the *I*, functioning both aesthetically and ethically, enables Trifonov to stand back while still making known his own opinions.

Trifonov uses the *I* for judgment in three ways. First, the *I* comments directly on the protagonist. The *I* in *Time and Place*, after initial resistance, likes his near double, Antipov, and says so. The *I* in *House on the Embankment*, who dislikes Glebov, seems trustworthy and reliable; he is a classmate who has no particular reason to love Glebov. His integrity is slightly compromised, however, by the jealousy that stems from his unrequited, furtive love for Sonia, who loves Glebov.[23] "In his memories [the *I*] tries to understand why she preferred someone whom he considers inferior and who does not reciprocate her feelings. The reader then has to be on guard against prejudices that might have entered this narrator's reflections."[24] Yet the *I* is still a reasonably good judge of character.

Second, judgment is implied in the intersecting perceptions of an incident. In both *House on the Embankment* and *Time and Place*, the *I*'s retrospective narration and the protagonist's of-the-time experience produce what one Soviet scholar calls "a zigzag pattern" of action. The result is a change in the relationship among parts of the work, an alteration in cause and effect. Motivations become clear only after we have already witnessed the actions thus motivated.[25]

Finally, judgment emerges not from the narrative voice per se but from structural juxtaposition and montage involving the episodes recounted by the *I*. In *House on the Embankment* those sections narrated by the *I* are inserted achronologically, at "crucial points in the main narration";[26] in them the *I* pays no special attention to Glebov, who is of much less interest to him than Sonia and Anton Ovchinnikov. But the careful placement of his narrative segments conveys a clear, if unspoken, evaluation of the action of the contiguous chapters, as the following examples illustrate.

The first interpolation of the *I* occurs after the protagonist, Vadim Glebov, describes a neighborhood battle. Lev Shulepnikov's stepfather, a high-ranking NKVD officer, gets rid of the clan that is terrorizing the street, the Bychkov family. Glebov's version reflects his own fear of violence and his awe of power. He stresses how the Bychkovs' dog ripped Lev and Anton's clothing, and how masterfully Levka's stepfather defeated this monstrous family. In the *I*'s account that follows, the dog's lunge and the beating are barely mentioned: it is Anton's bravery and his devastating skill at ju-jitsu that impressed the *I*. He recalls the "fabulous moments," when the attackers "fell instantly, without shouting, without struggling, as though of their own volition." Immediately afterward, in the resumed Glebov narration, Glebov gives Levka's stepfather the names of the boys who had attacked Lev months before. (Lev himself, no squealer, had refused to identify them.) The insertion of the first-person narrative just before the betrayal distances us from Glebov. It is a distance that continues to grow as Glebov grows up. "This collaboration of the reader at an ironic distance becomes essential for the transmission of Trifonov's meaning."[27]

The second passage narrated by the *I* interrupts events of a decade later, when Glebov is a graduate student at the Literary Institute. The anticosmopolitan campaign has begun, as has Glebov's involvement in the attacks on his thesis adviser and fiancée's father, Professor Ganchuk. The *I* takes us back to 1937 and a devilish test of nerve devised by Anton. The boys must prove their courage by walking on the far side of the balcony railing in the Ganchuks' ninth-floor apartment. The *I* describes his fear and his dependence on Anton. He characterizes Glebov as a man without qualities (*nikakoi chelovek*), someone onto whom people project whatever they want to see. In the balcony episode Glebov behaves precisely the way he will behave a dozen years later. All the boys are frightened, but only Glebov reveals the secret: he hints to Sonia that there will be something special to watch. He does not tell her what they are about to do, so technically he cannot be held responsible for interfering with the experiment. When she sees them and, horrified, shrieks at them to stop, the responsibility is all hers. Glebov even "snarls" at her for her interference. The *I* is both relieved to escape the danger and angry at Glebov for squealing. In the scenes of 1948 which succeed this episode, when Glebov prepares to betray his mentor as well as Sonia, he acts precisely the same way. He shifts responsibility away from himself for a betrayal he pretends is not a betrayal at all.

The last time the *I* sees Anton, Glebov, and Sonia is in 1941, during the evacuation of Moscow. The stability signified by the house on the embankment ended for the *I* in 1938. Now it is ending

for the others. He encounters new tenants in the building, benefi-
ciaries of apartments (like his) vacated by the purges. They insult
Sonia's German-born mother, barring her from the elevator and
making an offensive remark about "damn Germans." In the passage
that immediately follows the *I*'s narration Trifonov recounts Glebov's meeting in 1949 with Sonia's mother. In the wake of the campaign against her husband, Iuliia Mikhailovna has been dismissed
from her teaching job. While Glebov was not the instigator of the
persecution, or even a willing participant, his betrayal was the more
reprehensible because he was nearly a member of the family. Glebov
would never stoop to crass insults like the tenants during the war,
and he avoids confrontation at all costs. Yet he ends up doing Iuliia
Mikhailovna much greater harm than the malicious wartime neighbors, for she had reason to expect better of him.

In *Time and Place* the nameless narrator's life intersects the life
of the hero, Sasha Antipov, only twice. They work together at a
radiator factory in 1943–44; they meet again some thirty years later,
in the late 1970s, when the *I*'s daughter is treated for depression
by Antipov's physician son. The similarities between the two men
are emphasized: they are the same age, and both work in the factory
because they are too nearsighted to serve in the army. Both lost
their parents to the Stalinist maw, are hapless with women, and
dream of future success as writers. Indeed, the similarities are so
striking that at first the *I* dislikes Antipov: he senses in Antipov what
is bad in himself. At the same time those similarities allow, indeed
entitle, the anonymous narrator to pass judgment on Antipov when
his integrity is put to the test. Their fates "don't contradict each
other but [have] a certain mutual dependence or tie; one adds to
the other, illuminates it, continues it."[28]

The "test" confronting Antipov is typical for Trifonov's characters; it is a conflict between ethics and expediency. Antipov illegally obtains tobacco for his boss at the factory. He is caught, and
when he is interrogated he refuses to reveal the identity of the man
for whom he acquired the tobacco. The *I* narrator supports Antipov
and approves of his refusal to denounce the culprit, even as he be-
rates Antipov for his stubbornness. More telling, he emulates Antipov. Asked by an interrogator to confirm that the plant is riddled
with ideologically unreliable people, he behaves like Antipov—he

keeps silent. Both explicitly and tacitly, both verbally and in his actions, the *I* delivers a verdict on the protagonist, and that verdict is favorable.

The *I* also narrates two chapters that have nothing at all to do with Antipov. He recounts what happened to Agniia and Stas in 1938, and he describes the wartime evacuation of Moscow when he tried to help old family friends leave the city. He is therefore more than merely Sasha's peer and the judge of his behavior. He is, as well, a remembering consciousness. As such, he exemplifies another use Trifonov makes of the first-person voice.

I Remember . . .

At the beginning of *Time and Place* Trifonov poses a question: "Should one remember?" Initially he answers with a weary negative, but quickly he contradicts himself: "After all, to remember and to live—they are a unity, inseparable from each other, together forming some verb that has no name" (*TP* 205). In *The Old Man*, Letunov is both the recollector and a subject of recollection. In *Time and Place* the two roles are divided between Antipov and his occasional alter ego, the *I* who gets to know him during the war. Antipov lives experience; the *I* recalls experience. Because of this division *Time and Place* avoids the many flashbacks and major temporal jumps of *The Old Man*. Instead, it unfolds in a roughly chronological arrangement of chapters, interrupted only by chapters narrated by the *I*. Antipov lives exclusively in one tense: his "time" is always the present, while recollection is entrusted to the *I*, who lives in both the past and the present.[29]

In *Time and Place* Trifonov creates an *I* who in many ways replicates the narrator, and he gives some of his own experiences to Antipov, others to the *I*. Broadly, "the goal of this complex demarcation of the author, narrator and hero is . . . to express the commonality of fate among peers. This is why one can see, behind the intersections and crisscrossings, the campfire's reflection. The reflection of the historical campfire."[30] By his division of experience and perception Trifonov allows a generational "we" to emerge, much as Solzhenitsyn, in *One Day in the Life of Ivan Denisovich*, chose a narrative stance close to but not identical with the hero in order to produce a "generalized voice of the prisoners."[31] The combination of narrative modes banishes the traditional socialist realist objective narrator without replacing it by what Geoffrey Hosking calls "the mere individual, prisoner of his own consciousness."[32]

As part of that generational, historical voice, the *I* describes two deaths—the suicide of Agniia in 1938 and the death-in-life of Elizaveta Gavrilovna, the old lady paralyzed by a stroke who wants to be left behind to die during the wartime evacuation of Moscow. Usually when Trifonov's characters encounter mortality, through a brush with death or through the death of someone close, they are impelled to examine their own lives. In *Time and Place*, where death abuts life in each chapter, those deaths connected with Antipov's life—the fatal beating of a man of whom he is jealous, the suicide of his former teacher Kiianov—do spark introspection.[33] But the *I* is not directly affected by the deaths he mentions. In both cases he understands little because he is too young and cannot comprehend emotions so removed from his own experiences. Hence he functions as a recording consciousness; understanding is left to the reader.

What we understand is that both women have been forced by the times into intolerable situations from which death alone can liberate them. The paralyzed Elizaveta Gavrilovna, remembering how she handed a revolver to a revolutionary comrade whose wife and child had died, wishes for similar help, yet her paralysis is so severe that she cannot communicate her wishes even to those who love her most, her daughter and her granddaughter.

Agniia, on the other hand, has death within her power. Her suicide follows her husband's recovery from a lengthy depression, during which Stas had spent his days lying on his bed, his face turned to the wall. All noise, all manifestations of normal life irritated him; his illness consisted, the narrator reflects, of "wanting nothing." His "work," scribblings on the history of Neskuchnoi Garden and the First City Hospital of Moscow, had been construed as a symptom of his illness. Stas's depression (like David Shvarts's mental illness in *The Disappearance*) suggests a reaction to circumstances, an evasion of an intolerable reality.

The narrator, only eleven or twelve years old at the time, understood neither Stas's depression nor his recovery, and as an adult he thinks that too many years have passed to get to the bottom of the truth. But the logical inference to be drawn from what he describes is that Agniia's suicide was caused by her husband's infatuation with Minka, the girl she had brought into her own home. Agniia's death has no direct link with the political terror of the time, but the destructive force of the era is symbolized by the destruction of the ersatz family Agniia has manufactured out of leftover bits of other families.

In *Time and Place*, as in *House on the Embankment*, the first-person narrative interpolations often begin with the words "I remember," adding to the narrative a lyric dimension, the "element of memory, alive and not subordinate to the shattering effect of time."[34] Like the *I* in *House on the Embankment* and Sanka Izvarin in *The Old Man*, the *I* in *Time and Place* combines with other voices to produce a polyphonic fictional imitation of the layering of time which exists in life. It thus becomes another weapon against forgetting.[35] Trifonov pits the memory of the first-person narrator against the idea (which, expressed by Glebov, is also a fervent wish) that "whatever one didn't remember ceased to exist." Suffering does not vanish without a trace. "If someone remembers," one of his characters says, "that means that it happened." Memory and retrospection bestow understanding. If characters do not necessarily perceive the meaning of an event when it happens, they sometimes come to understand after it is past.

The stories of *The Overturned House*, written at about the same time as *Time and Place*, are all narrated by a first-person voice that—like Letunov—at once recollects the past and is, in varying degrees, the subject of recollection. The storyteller's voice is familiar, its inflections elegiac. Its timbre recalls the historian, epic and retrospective, who introduces *House on the Embankment*: "Not one of those boys is alive today. Some were killed in the war, some died from sickness, some disappeared without a trace, while others, still alive, have turned into different people; and if by some magic means those different people were to meet their past selves ... they would no longer know what to say to them. I fear, in fact, that they would not even guess they were meeting themselves" (*HE* 189).

Trifonov regularly used a single first-person voice in short pieces; their brevity does not support multiple narrators. But the *I* of the stories in *Overturned House* is unexpectedly melancholy. "Nothing astounds me," he says in "Cats or Hares," "and I don't really feel like writing. . . . Life is a gradual loss of the astounding." The *I* speaks of an ebbing of life, a loss of energy and wonder, of hope. The intimacy of this voice and what Ivanova calls its "vulnerable openness" approach confessional. It signals a shift in Trifonov's fictional stance. In these last stories he is moving away from pure aesthetics, from belletristic narrative, for the sake of ethics. He is addressing an open monologue to the reader, in which he articulates his position and worldview.[36]

Trifonov's turn toward confession suggests something close to despair. The crippling intransigence and stultification of Soviet society in the 1970s may have bred in Trifonov a rejection of the expansive, social forms of fiction such as novellas and novels, and a dissatisfaction with the masks of fictional personae. He wanted to speak in his own voice; he no longer saw possibility beyond the self.[37]

Trifonov was not alone in moving toward a less mediated relationship with the reader. A. Mikhailov, discussing the increase in short, one-idea stories in the early 1980s, observes that "the writer tries to get at the reader's conscience, to destroy the remnants of his civic peace of mind and complacency as quickly as possible. And what gives . . . the opportunity for this is the short, nonfiction story, most often in the first person, about what's most important, what torments the writer, what keeps him awake at night." Animated by a lyric-confessional tone, an intensified authenticity, this prose depicts "a man's inner life and the experience of his soul," the author's relationship with the world.[38]

Whether in the more conventional fiction of the novellas and the novels or in the almost unmediated self-expression of *The Overturned House*, Trifonov exploited similar narrative strategies to articulate his point of view. In his mature works the functions and roles of these strategies multiplied as his style increasingly bore the burden of his ideas. The same is true for Trifonov's use of chronotopes, the subject of the next chapter.

VI

Byt

I n at least one respect art replicates memory. Both have the power
to defeat time's destructive force because both are able to recreate the past. Art operates as memory does, choosing and sorting,
winnowing significant from meaningless. But memory's net is often
cast beyond conscious choice, while art—first and fundamentally
artifice—is always a matter of deliberate decisions. In one of his last
stories Trifonov wrote that "memory like the artist picks out details.
There is nothing whole, nothing unified [*slitnyi*] in memory, but
then it strikes sparks. . . . The feelings disappeared long ago, carried
off like litter by the wind, but then a detail, forged of steel, glitters:
swinging on the swing in the garden."[1]

As an artist, Trifonov imitated the dowser who can detect the
presence of water beneath a seemingly solid surface. He traced the
network of underground pipes through which the "dead" past flows;
he charted the movement within it. Just as Antipov, the writer-hero
of *Time and Place*, tries to examine the past by means of his novel
within a novel, so Trifonov—more accomplished an artist than Antipov—used his art to examine and reanimate the past via Bakh-
tinian "chronotopes": "In the literary artistic chronotope, spatial
and temporal indicators are fused into one carefully thought-out,
concrete whole. Time, as it were, thickens, takes on flesh, becomes
artistically visible; likewise, space becomes charged and responsive
to the movements of time, plot and history."[2]

Such "time-space patterns" are signposts on a road map leading
to the heart of Trifonov's concerns: the relationship of time and

place as the matrix of moral choice. Writing against a background of rigidly defined and instantly recognizable chronotopes, Trifonov could and did manipulate them in order to alert readers to a very different set of values. As Katerina Clark explains, "Since Stalinist socialist realism offered writers a ready-made system of signs with fixed political meanings, it had the potential to be used as a sort of Aesopian language, a medium for writers to express themselves— even if only in a very tentative way—on politically delicate subjects.... Much [post-Stalin] fiction manages to [provide myths for maintaining the status quo] while also manipulating the clichés of the socialist realist tradition for oblique self-expression."[3] The nexus of time and place as matrix of moral choice does not in itself violate the limits of the permissible in Soviet fiction. What does violate them is the way Trifonov perceived and presented that matrix, specifically his use of *byt*.

Byt

Byt is conventionally defined as "way of life" and is distinguished from the word *bytie*, a philosophical term denoting "being," "existence," or "objective reality." As an example of the latter the *Oxford Russian-English Dictionary* offers: "*existence* determines consciousness." The adjectival form *bytovoi* is rendered as "social," with *bytovaia revoliutsiia* (social revolution) the example, but also as "everyday," as in *bytovaia p'esa* (a play on the theme of everyday life) and *bytovoe iavlenie* (everyday occurrence). Ushakov's classic 1935 Russian dictionary defines *byt* as "general style of life characteristic of a certain social group," giving "everyday life" as a secondary meaning. *Bytie* is defined as "existence, reality." Perhaps the clearest distinction defines *byt* as the everyday routine sufficient unto itself, and *bytie* as existence, or objective reality, which includes the everyday manifestations of that reality.[4]

The distinction between *byt* (*realia*) and *bytie* (*realiora*) has a long history in the Russian intellectual tradition that continued into the Soviet period.[5] In the literary debates of the post-Stalin years the concept of *bytovaia literatura* has assumed exceptional significance because, by focusing on the "everyday," it implicitly rejects the ultimate purpose, the transcendent Goal, which buttresses teleological socialist realist literature. Reality is seen, and presented, not "in the light of its revolutionary development" but for itself and its immanent meaning. Thus the final end of history, no longer known ahead of time, is replaced with "openness to experience, with close, even loving attention to things and people immediately [at hand]."[6]

Bytopisanie—that is, depicting everyday life stripped of its larger social (and socialist) context—was a serious charge leveled at a number of popular writers in the 1960s and 1970s. The popular novelist I. Grekova, for instance, recalls that she was often criticized for "excessive attention to the daily routine ('pedestrian description of everyday trifles')."[7] Trifonov was attacked with particular ferocity after the publication of the Moscow trilogy and *Another Life*.[8] But the charge cropped up regularly, and it came to irritate Trifonov. Toward the end of his life he responded to a question about *byt* with some heat. *Bytovaia* literature as such does not exist, he said. "The senseless concept *byt* simply confuses things; like a bottomless pit it takes in all aspects and manifestations of human life. I write about death (*The Exchange*)—I'm told that I'm writing about *byt*; I write about love (*The Long Goodbye*)—they say it's again about *byt*; I write about a family falling apart (*Taking Stock*)—again I hear about *byt*."[9]

His interviewer, Lev Anninskii, countered that saying that one writes "about love" or "about death" is no more helpful as a defining rubric than writing "about *byt*." The objection is fair. But it fails to come to grips with the function of *byt* for Trifonov, especially in his mature works. Anninskii sees the combination of *byt* and *intelligentsiia* as paradoxical: the very notion of *intelligentsiia* suggests overcoming *byt*, the detritus and circumstances of "base nature," yet the only context within which the spirit can be realized is in those very ordinary circumstances—"in that damnable, oppressive *byt*." Anninskii dismisses Trifonov's "angry philippics" as being a protest against the *word*, not the concept: "Trifonov cannot throw out the word '*byt*,' because *byt* is a form of existence [*bytie*], but neither can he accept it because it is a false form of existence, a profanation of spiritual reality."[10]

The meaning of *byt* in Trifonov's later fiction becomes clearer if we consider it not as the subject of his work but as a multifunctional aesthetic device within it. Trifonov does not merely reproduce or render *byt*. He freights it, so that characteristic details become symbolic and carry emotional tension.[11] As one of the most thoughtful Soviet critics has observed, every genre—war prose, village prose, industrial prose, *bytovaia* prose—can produce literature of thematic pettiness, fiction that reflects everyday life to the smallest detail but lacks a defined, meaningful artistic ideal; equally, however, every genre can rise above such limitations.[12]

In Trifonov's case, *byt* first enables him to reproduce the reality of a specific era; in that sense it performs in the service of naturalism. Second, *byt* is linked with the movement of time itself: it creates a sense of context, temporal no less than social, within which particular lives are led. The everyday manifestations of a given era are not removed from the flow of historical time but are interwoven with that flow, separate yet simultaneous. They are not stagnant, "the frozen existence of dead things,"[13] but create a fully tangible, plastic image of historical time. Some of Trifonov's characters are able to recognize the connection between history and the detritus of everyday life; many are not. But Trifonov's readers are constantly forced to recognize the interdependence of the two, in large part because of the complex network of *bytovye* details.[14]

Within that network, places are particularly important and houses command special attention. For Trifonov's characters, houses often serve as the "magic point of crystallization" for memories.[15] For Trifonov's readers, they are multivalent hieroglyphs that become increasingly complex as Trifonov's work matures. They therefore merit careful examination.

The House I Live In

In *The Exchange*, set in the late 1960s, housing is first of all a quotidian concern. The acute housing shortage that has plagued Moscow ever since the war gives the novella its name: on a literal level the "exchange" referred to is the apartment exchange the hero's wife, Lena, is trying to arrange now that her mother-in-law is dying. Concrete details are given full weight. Thus we learn that Dmitriev's mother lives in a "nice twenty-by-sixteen [meter] room on Profsoiuznaia Street"; that is, a spacious room in a desirable location. Lena has her eye on a two-room apartment on Malaia Gruzinskaia, also in a choice location and with double their present space.[16] We learn that obtaining a decent apartment requires a great deal of maneuvering, possibly with the help of an agent, and extra incentive, often a cash premium, to interest the other party. It might even involve a third apartment and an extra exchange.

Tension throbs between husband and wife. Dmitriev is upset because after years of strained relations, Lena is now willing to live with his mother only because she is dying and her death will enable them to get a better apartment. Lack of space enforces their intimacy as it confines their quarrels to whispers: their daughter is asleep behind a curtain. Dmitriev is angry at Lena's tactless but well-founded confidence that he will go along with her plan. His anger is expressed in his abrupt exit from their room, rendered via verbs and adverbs: he *jumps* up from the chair *with a jerk*, *grabs* his towel, *runs* from the room. He doesn't want to accept the hostility between the two women, Lena's ruthlessness, and his mother's imminent death. He avoids confronting any of these realities, hiding behind prosaic, *bytovye* questions. In just this way he has avoided recognizing the exchange of values that has imperceptibly occurred over the course of his married life.

Both the lack of adequate housing and the dwellings themselves are mentioned in relation to nearly every character in the book. Hence housing acts first of all to create a literal picture of Moscow society: the size of its rooms, the quality of its furniture, the pictures on its walls, the contents of its cupboards. Further, housing is part of the hierarchies—of values and power—within the society. Information about housing is a commodity to be bartered. While most of Dmitriev's colleagues freely share their housing experiences with him, one man withholds information about how to effect a successful exchange because the potential return is not worthwhile; Dmitriev has nothing to offer.

A house should signify a home. Both characters and readers perceive the house to be the proper locus for love and intimacy, but more often than not it conspicuously fails to contain them. In *Taking Stock*, for example, Gennadii Sergeevich and his family live in a spacious apartment, "sixty-two square meters of living space, not including the storage area," opulent and attractive but completely devoid of warmth. In *The Exchange*, similarly, Dmitriev's former mistress, Tania, has a large and luxurious apartment. Though their affair ended three years earlier, Tania still loves Dmitriev and does not wish to live with her husband. Her rooms, still only half furnished three years after she moved in, are unkempt, like her emotionally bereft life.

In its early years the Dmitriev family dacha held both love and warmth. When Dmitriev's father built the dacha in the 1930s it was a center of activity for adults and children. Now it is a relic, emptied actually and metaphorically. Of the "nests, tribes with their environment, conversation, games, and music," only Dmitriev's mother and, temporarily, his sister remain. Even the natural environment has disappeared. A concrete embankment replaces what used to be Dmitriev's favorite sandy river slope, and a manmade beach complete with cabanas, deck chairs, and kiosks has taken over what once was a meadow. The first happy year of Dmitriev's marriage was spent at the dacha, where he lived with Lena, her parents, his mother, and his grandfather. The new paint and wallpaper adorning the dacha, paid for by loans from his in-laws, were a sign of the early (and short-lived) amicability between the two families. Often in Trifonov's works chunks of time are compressed into morsels of place: the described place remains part of the hero's consciousness although the moment itself rushes past and disappears.[17] For Dmitriev, the joy of that early period is recalled and reified in visual terms: where each person slept in the dacha, the veranda where they all drank tea. "It had been like that, for sure. It had been, it had been. Only it didn't stay in his memory, it rushed past, vanished, because he couldn't live for anything, or see anyone but Lena" (E 64–65). That life vanished long ago, and by the end of The Exchange so has the dacha colony itself.

The house, in the Moscow trilogy and in Another Life, functions first as a medium of information, explicit or implied, about postwar Soviet society and its cramped lack of privacy. Second, it becomes an emblem of the disjunction between professional success and personal happiness. Trifonov's characters believe that by acquiring more space, by moving out of a room in a communal apartment into a private apartment, they and their families will be happier. There is, in fact, no instance where this actually occurs. Gennadii Sergeevich and Rita shared more in the crowded communal apartment they lived in when they were first married than they do in their sixty-two square meters. In Time and Place, Antipov and Tania, after years of lack of space and privacy, finally move into a new, large apartment near Moscow's Aeroport Metro station when the region is being built up in the late 1960s and early 1970s. They hope the move will trigger or create or carry in its wake a renewal of their marriage. They themselves don't know what the relationship between a new home and a new stage in their marriage might be; they only hope that there will be one. It doesn't work. Sasha and Tania were far closer to each other in the quarters they shared with Tania's relative in the early 1950s than they are now. They were young then, and their life together was filled with possibilities.

Trifonov never identifies lack of space and overcrowding as a source of happiness, and a number of his characters are unhappy in their communal apartments. But he does suggest that diagnosing the cause of a psychological or emotional problem as lack of space is an error which leads to a greater error—the delusion that the problem can be solved by more space. Most of his heroes were born in the 1920s, so they came of age after the war, when the housing shortage was most acute. Their early adult years, replete with hope and possibility and the first years of marriage, coincided with their having to live with relatives or in single rooms. By the time they are successful and prosperous enough to move—and there are bigger apartments available for them to rent or even buy—they have moved into new phases of their lives, often coincident with marital dissatisfaction, professional disappointment, spiritual restlessness, or fatigue. In *The Exchange* the housing exchange signifies Dmitriev's gradual abandonment of the "Dmitriev" standards (essentially those of the intelligentsia, comprising disinterest, idealism, and a disdain for compromise) for the "Lukianov" standards (essentially those of the *meshchantsvo*, comprising pragmatism, materialism, and an ability to get things done). Thus the dwellings—the dacha and the apartments—become symbols of moral choice.

Window on the Past

In the later works—*House on the Embankment, The Old Man, Time and Place, The Disappearance,* and the stories of *Overturned House*—houses continue to fulfill the two functions of conveying information and symbolizing moral choice. In addition, they become the chief physical representation of the lost past and a constantly shifting marker of time. "Most often man bumps into history in his everyday existence, without recognizing the presence of history in that existence, without understanding, for instance, that the official furniture in the house on the embankment with which his parents set up the apartment is also history. And those little houses in which Trifonov's heroes can find neither warmth nor comfort are not merely *byt*, but a piece of history."[18]

In *Time and Place*, when Kiianov's old friend Teterin returns to Moscow from exile in the early 1950s, Kiianov is in the same building, even the same apartment, he occupied twenty years earlier, while Teterin must scuffle around trying to acquire a Moscow residence permit. No wonder Teterin shies away from coming to that house, that apartment: to meet there would suggest that nothing had occurred—not Teterin's arrest, not his years in prison, camp, and exile. No wonder he prefers the impersonality of a crowded public place.

In *Time and Place* the normal fixed solidity of place loses its hard edges, deconstructs into the ambiguity of moving time. The paradox is inherent in the very title. Nothing could seem more stable than place, yet the places of *Time and Place*, the neighborhoods of Moscow, disappear; nothing is more mobile than time, yet thanks to memory and art time can be held—not frozen, perhaps, but not lost either.[19]

Throughout the novel, movement is contrasted with stasis. In the chapter describing the evacuation of Moscow during the war, the contrast is internalized in the character of a stroke victim. Like one of Dante's sinners in the circle of ice at the bottom of hell, this former revolutionary is reduced to communicating by blinks of her eye. Yet though her body is condemned to a total absence of motion, her mind ranges freely through time. When Stalin dies, Antipov's elderly neighbor, Veretennikova, never budges from her balcony while the crowds on the streets below surge toward the Kremlin. Antipov's teacher Kiianov is consistently depicted as sitting or lying. Ever the observer, never the participant, Kiianov ends by committing suicide, the last denial of movement.[20]

In the penultimate chapter, entitled "Time and Place" and set in 1978, Antipov himself embodies stasis. Fifty-two years old, he has lived alone since his divorce five years earlier. One child is emotionally distant, the other geographically far away. His mother is dead. He has "freed himself" of vanity, of the power of women, of the egoism of friends. He has sold his books and furniture. He suffers from the indifference T. S. Eliot describes in "Little Gidding":

> There are three conditions which often look alike
> Yet differ completely, flourish in the same hedgerow:
> Attachment to self and to things and to persons,
>   detachment
> From self and from things and from persons; and, growing
>   between them, indifference
> Which resembles the others as death resembles life . . .

Whenever it appears in Trifonov's work, this anomie is a symptom of something profoundly wrong. It is the same condition that keeps Agniia's husband, Stas, in bed, facing the wall and unable to tolerate any noise. It is same illness that afflicts the first-person narrator's daughter in the last chapter of *Time and Place*, preventing her from enjoying even her baby son. Antipov lies around his empty apartment, not reading, not thinking, not watching soccer on television. He tries to tune out the vicarious life brought him by his old friend Markusha, the incarnation of perpetual motion, who is forever coming and going. He is unwilling to participate in the everyday *realia*, the *byt* of life.

In *House on the Embankment* the house itself becomes the central expression of that curious, paradoxical connection between time and place. The house connotes, and conjures up, the vanished life of the nameless narrator at the time when his family and his world are destroyed by the 1937–38 purges. For the protagonist, Vadim Glebov, the imposing house on the embankment is one end of the physical axis of his childhood, the other end of which is his own small, shabby building which stands in its shadow. Together they evoke the network of Moscow subsocieties: the intellectual elite represented by the Ganchuk family, the party/NKVD elite of Levka's mother and stepfather, the twentieth-century "poor folk" embodied in Glebov's beaten-down father. The corrosive envy experienced by the have-nots is strong in Glebov. He fiercely resents the residents of the house, and he identifies the spoiled, carelessly generous Levka as a typical inhabitant, even though a very different child, Anton, also lives there.

In the novella the house is, as it was in reality, occupied by members of the government and party elite, people like Levka's stepfather (and Trifonov's father).[21] For Glebov it is the glittering prize, symbol of what he desperately wants to attain and become. Years later, when he first makes love to Sonia Ganchuk, his desire for her is spurred by a sudden sense of possession of a dwelling, in this case the Ganchuk dacha:

> ... he lay on the divan, an old-fashioned one with bolsters and a tasseled fringe, put his hands behind his head, stared at the ceiling with its striped wallpaper darkened with age, at the strips of insulating felt that poked out between the planking of the walls, which were adorned with photographs and a little engraving of a scene from the Russo-Turkish War, and suddenly—like a rush of blood to the head, making him dizzy—he had the feeling that all this might become his house. Even now, perhaps—no one had guessed it yet, but he knew—these yellowing boards with their knotholes and photographs, the squeaky window frame, the snow-covered roof *belonged to him*. (HE 260)

Glebov's possession of Sonia's body is linked explicitly, consciously, with ownership of the house: "There was no weight in this body, but now it belonged to him—or so he felt; it belonged to him along with everything else: the old house, the fir trees, the snow."

The ghost of the past, Levka Shulepnikov, reappears in Glebov's present in connection with housing. Glebov runs into Shulepnikov when he is on the trail of antiques for his new apartment. Levka is consistently associated with houses. In childhood it is the enormous apartment in the house on the embankment; after the war, during the anticosmopolitan campaign, it is the apartment where he and his mother watch television (available at that time to only a handful of ultraprivileged individuals). Appropriate to the downward trajectory of Lev's life, his final appearance in the novella is as gatekeeper of the cemetery where Sonia is buried, next to an old, disused crematorium, a house of the dead. He is "a constant reminder of a past from which Glebov can never really free himself."[22]

In 1972, the present of *House on the Embankment*, the house is physically still standing,[23] but it has been displaced as the symbol of Glebov's status and the concrete sign of all he has achieved by other houses, such as the dacha where he received Levka's phone call. Glebov has tried to expunge the image of that house. When, however, Levka activates the force of memory, the power that the house had in the past and its hold on Glebov—out of which, on top of which, Glebov's success has grown—appear to be undiminished.[24]

The same house on the embankment plays a central role in *The Disappearance*.[25] In this novella, unpublished during Trifonov's lifetime, the metaphor of the house functions much as it does in his other, published, works, but it refers much more explicitly to the 1937 purges. The title itself, the narrator states, denotes the disappearance of everything signified by the house he lived in as a child except its shell, its physical structure: "It died long ago, when I left it. That's what happens with houses: we abandon them and they die" (D 7). This is the house the hero, Igor, dreams of when he is sixteen and returns from evacuation in Tashkent to a war-emptied Moscow—the house and "the old apartment where we lived before, with father" (D 10), its rooms, mirrors, and wall decorations re-created in photographic and loving detail.

The intensification of fear as the Stalinist terror worsens is conveyed in *The Disappearance* primarily through images of the house on the embankment and four of its apartments. Two are paired as contrasts: the apartment of David Shvarts, a once-powerful Old Bolshevik, now superannuated, and the flat triumphantly occupied by Arsenii Florinskii, once a nonentity but now a powerful figure in the NKVD. Florinskii is at the top of the new heap; Shvarts, though nominally respected, is actually on the bottom, no longer a factor to be taken into account. The other two flats belong to Igor's family, the Baiukovs, and to a high-level *apparatchik* and his wife. Both families are in imminent danger. The Baiukovs are doomed because they are honorable vestiges of an irrelevant idealism. The *apparatchik* is doomed because he is a loyal servant of a regime that devours its own: he will inevitably be fed to the same machine he serves. Hence, in *The Disappearance* the house on the embankment becomes more than the backdrop of the purges and the symbol of what disappears. In its very warp and woof it is part of the Terror, physically and atmospherically, and its four apartments form a microcosm of those who implemented and those who fell victim to the purges.

House of Cards

In 1936, on the eve of the phase of the Great Terror that swept away the Soviet political and army elite, the Baiukov family consists of eleven-year-old Igor, or Gorik, his sister, his parents, his maternal grandmother, and his mother's brother Sergei. It is his father's first real home. He has lived in many places, but only now, living with his wife and children, does he have a home. (Several years later, his son unknowingly echoes his father's definition of home. Wandering through wartime Moscow, Igor senses that there is no home for him in the whole huge city because none of his family is there. His home is in a place he has never been, Kazakhstan, where his mother is serving out her term of exile.) Yet for Nikolai Grigorevich Baiukov, "home" also signifies a political and social reality, which he has fought to create and to which he has pledged his life. The apartment he shares with Liza and their family, their personal home, is dependent on their larger home, the Soviet state. Indeed, the former is unthinkable without the latter. What is happening now, in 1937, puts at risk both homes. In his gloom, as he thinks about his and Liza's home (a home "for the sake of which revolutions are fought"), it seems very frail. "It suddenly occurred to him, with momentary and mad force, that this whole pyramid of comforts glittering in the night, this Tower of Babel made out of lampshades, was also temporary, would also fly away like ashes in the wind" (D 39).

For the child Gorik, home is safe and secure, a source of love and stability. Yet day by day the world is becoming more abnormal and more unstable, and his father cannot prevent or slow the process. The house seems to shake with fear; the weak are afraid for themselves, the strong are afraid for the people they love. When Gorik's uncle Serezha visits his mistress Ada one night, in another section of the house, he first goes to a friend's apartment to protect Ada's reputation. On the threshold stands his friend's mother, her skin splotched with fear: "Volodicheva didn't say a word, but her whole stricken appearance cried out: 'What is it? Say it! But if it's something awful you shouldn't have, you didn't have the right . . .'" (D 77).

Ada's husband is a weak man turned aggressive by fear. His long-time respect for David Shvarts is transformed into snarling name-calling; a friend who jokingly refers to Stalin's height becomes the butt of his fear-driven fury. When Ada's doorbell rings at 3:45 A.M., a silent, efficient NKVD team enters to search the apartment. The NKVD men are businesslike, indifferently brushing off Ada's query about her husband's whereabouts: "he's where he belongs." Ada, unafraid for herself, is full of fear for her husband; Serezha, also unafraid for himself, fears for his mother. After three hours the search is over, the den sealed off. As the NKVD unit prepares to depart, one officer chats to Serezha as he washes his hands, casually complaining that because of the press of work he's hardly seen his wife all week.

The Disappearance draws to a nonclosure ending in a continuing counterpoint of routine and fear. Every knock at Gorik's apartment evokes dread because it is so obviously only a matter of time before his father is arrested. Meanwhile his father persists in trying to preserve the pretense of normalcy despite the disappearance every day of familiar faces in the office dining room. He wants to compel recognition of the peril—and at the same time hold on to the illusion of his home's stability. When, finally, the doorbell rings after midnight, he is ready, dressing quickly but with clumsy fingers that can't quite manipulate the shirt buttons. It happens that the caller turns out to be his nephew, not the NKVD—this time. But both Nikolai Grigorevich and the reader know that it's merely a fluke. Sooner or later, the expected visitors will arrive.

The Disappearance ends with an image of Gorik secure in the loving home that surrounds him, secure even in his father's annoyance at some mischief. His mother promises that his father's irritation will certainly pass; she tucks the blanket closer around him. But that conclusion is no more than a pause, a breath drawn in and released before the "real" action resumes. As Gorik himself senses, his home is not stable. Inevitably, inexorably, its dissolution is approaching.

House and Homeland

For the characters given the core of Trifonov's life story—Gorik, the anonymous narrator in *House on the Embankment*, Sanka Izvarin in *The Old Man*—the house signifies security and love; eviction from it signals the disappearance of both. For Trifonov, by the end of his life, the house image came ultimately to symbolize Russia itself. In his last story cycle, *The Overturned House*, the house has rocked so far that it has toppled over. The narrator of the title story comments that whenever he goes far away from home he sees his "overturned, fragmented house," and he means not merely a specific dacha but his larger home—his nation.

In each of the stories included in *Overturned House* Trifonov writes about Russia in the context of travel and emigration.[26] "In the moon's landscape, within its craters, its multistoried castles ... I see my house, but in upside-down form. As if reflected, blurrily, in water." The "blurring" of Russia's image in these stories comes from two lenses, one lent by distance, the other by time. All the stories describe times spent outside Russia, but Trifonov "domesticizes" the exotica of the world. He links foreign locations and sights with those at home, so that rank fish in an Italian square remind him of fish in a particular Moscow grocery, and girls garlanded with coin trays in a Las Vegas casino remind him of long-gone cigarette vendors on Tverskoi Boulevard. More important, his foreign experiences lead him home again, to Russia and to himself. The foreign sites of the stories form an avenue for self-analysis, for the labor of self-consciousness. "Eternity—history—contemporaneity; these are the coordinates of the stories whose action takes place in Rome, in Sicily."[27]

Emigration is not inevitably catastrophic, although until recently it was effectively irreversible for Soviets who left their homeland. In "A Visit to Marc Chagall" Trifonov shows us how Chagall took his home with him, triumphantly re-creating Vitebsk in drawings and on canvas. But in "Eternal Themes" and "Death in Sicily" emigration means alienation, a bitter loss of home. In the former story Trifonov encounters a onetime editor in the Phoenix Hotel in Rome, an appropriate place to find figures resurrected from the past. The man (not named, but known from Trifonov's reminiscences to be the former *Novyi mir* editor Boris Zaks) explains sourly that he and his third wife are bound for America, where her children and grandchildren live. He resents leaving his old father in Russia; he resents his wife's "unnatural" love for her children; he blames his own professional setbacks on her former husband, for the sake of whose grandchild he had to abandon Russia.

His dissatisfaction is a product as much of his own personality as of circumstances. He carries his rancor with him and was hardly different years before, when he brusquely rejected a manuscript Trifonov submitted because it was about "eternal themes."[28] The longer they speak, the more spiteful the editor becomes, linking the two of them as disappointed, disillusioned old men. "Do you still hope to astound the world?" he asks, rhetorically but with the intent of inflicting pain. "Do you think the world will stop in its tracks for reading your opus?" His face, empty "as an old Italian square at twilight," takes on the familiar expression of a "sad executioner." Trifonov pities him. The two men may both be aging, as the editor insists, but they are not in the same position. The writer is in Italy by choice; he can and will go home again. The editor is in the West against his wishes and has no hope of returning home. The once-rebuffed writer is still writing about the "eternal themes" and still has readers; the once-powerful editor is now without occupation or purpose.

For Signora Maddaloni, the émigré writer in "Death in Sicily," the half century she has spent outside Russia seems less meaningful than her first two decades in Russia. She shares with Trifonov the few bits of paper that represent her Russian past: photos of her mother and of herself as a child, and official documents. She and Trifonov have in common the Russian language, a point underscored during their conversation by the silence of the narrator's "guide" and Signora Maddaloni's servant, neither of whom understands a word of what the two writers are saying.

Signora Maddaloni's family history is Trifonov's family history inverted, "overturned." She was in Novocherkassk during the Civil War, when his uncle was military commandant there. Her family was pro-White and emigrated, his family was pro-Bolshevik and stayed. The political sympathies of the two families were diametrically opposed, but the fates of both were fashioned by politics. She comments that the worst thing of all is to have to die in Sicily. Without bitterness but with sadness Signora Maddaloni acknowledges that she—like the editor in "Eternal Themes"—has lost her home. To die alone, away from one's homeland and roots, is a hard fate.

Trifonov seems to be making the point that death, not emigration, is the bitter reality. For the shadow of death that hovers over Signora Maddaloni in her Sicilian exile is no less devastating when it falls on Trifonov's friend Boris, at home in Russia, in the title story. (Boris is modeled on the translator and essayist Lev Ginzburg, who died in 1980.) His death suggests another meaning of the house image: a man's life, upended and destroyed, as Boris's life is shattered unexpectedly. Death strikes him like lightning, like a whirlwind.

Trifonov writes "The Overturned House" in part for him, though Boris—he thinks—would not be interested in a story about Las Vegas, let alone the sights Trifonov saw in America: a Kansas rodeo, a Russian professor with the extraordinary name of Tamerlane Chingiskhanovich (who wears light blue suits and drives a light blue Cadillac), bread with the consistency and taste of cotton, drunken Indians, and the "biggest horse in the world," on view for twenty-five cents. Boris would have been indifferent: "he didn't want to hear about anything, because he knew it anyway. He knew everything very well, without America and without me. So it seemed to him."

Trifonov suggests, with weariness and love, that Boris would have been wrong. These wondrous, if occasionally bizarre, American scenes are no more irrelevant than the familiar garlic- and onion-strung veranda they sat on twenty years earlier, its floor scattered with overripe tomatoes. "For some reason it seems to me that everything is related to everything. Everything living is connected." Or, as one American with a Russian surname replies to Trifonov's question about kin in Moscow, "Everyone in this world is my relation." Cutting across differences of time and place are universal human needs and fears, attempts to control fate, attempts to evade death.

In "The Overturned House" Trifonov describes Soviets who played cards together on a dacha veranda in the mid-1950s and Americans who gamble and quarrel and love in casinos and hotels in the mid-1970s. They could hardly have less in common. Yet despite the many and genuine differences, "then" and "now," "here" and "there," "they" and "we" are closer than either group might think: each is an upside-down image of the other, blurred but recognizable. Both the Russians in 1954 and the Americans in 1976 believe they can control their fates. When Trifonov, Boris, and Lieutenant Gusev sit up until dawn, ostensibly playing cards but actually playing with possibility, they are "stupefied" with the notion of "changing fate." Stalin is dead (we understand without being explicitly told); at long last the times are changing. "Great possibilities have no measure, they have only a smell, a wind that chills the soul." More than twenty years later, when few of the hoped-for changes have materialized, the dacha card game is unexpectedly reflected in the casinos of Las Vegas, where crowds feed one-armed bandits in another attempt to control destiny. "All this was not like Repikhovo [the dacha colony]. But some sort of thread—I could feel it—connected these two spots ... [a thread of] love, death, hopes, disappointments, despair and happiness brief as a gust of wind."

The Americans in the Las Vegas casino are confident, even arrogant. Trifonov is told that Americans love successful people, hence they like optimistic literature and lose patience with Russian "losers." But what they believe and what they experience are contradictory. One woman loves "lucky" people and thinks people make their own destiny; if they fail, they have somehow deserved to fail. Her daughter, however, is a hysterical neurotic, and the scripts her lover writes are repeatedly turned down. Another, who twice quotes Henley's poetic cliché of man as forger of his happiness and master of his fate, finds happiness to be short-lived indeed.

On the Repikhovo veranda and in Las Vegas, people hope and believe they are masters of their fates. Misfortune is not a meaningful concept to Trifonov's characters. Whether Russian or American, they regard experience as a form of test or trial, not as an unhappy turn of the wheel of Fortune to be endured blindly, uncomprehendingly.[29] Yet their fates happen to them unpredictably, before they are ready or when they are thinking of something else entirely. The fourth man on the veranda, who confirmed what Trifonov had only guessed about the purges, died unexpectedly two years later; Boris, hardly ill, died before Trifonov could visit him. All that people *can* control is how they react to what happens to them.

The last story in *The Overturned House*, "Grey Sky, Masts and a Chestnut Horse," offers a reflection of home blurred by time. It suggests an old-fashioned glass paperweight which creates the illusion of a snowstorm when shaken. The title refers to one of Trifonov's few memories of the early childhood years he spent in Finland, when his father was Soviet trade representative there. On a trip to Finland he retrieves a distant memory, the title image of sky, masts, and a horse in the snow, and is stunned to have the accuracy of his memory confirmed by an old lady who remembers the horse: it was called Cally and it belonged to a laundryman named Anderson.

"Grey Sky, Masts and a Chestnut Horse" captures a paradox: the reality of the past is discrete and irretrievable, yet art has the power to link past and present. Trifonov recalls how he returned to his family's dacha during the war and found their skis missing. When he did locate one pair, in a neighbor's shed, he left it there. The skis were symbolic of the life that had existed and vanished, the family that had existed and was destroyed; it would have been pointless to take them. On the June morning when his father vanished, Trifonov felt a mixture of foreboding and giddy liberation, for he was finally free to play with some Finnish knives that had been off-limits until then. In time the knives disappeared, like the Finnish sled and the school notebooks mentioned in another story, and like the people: his stepbrother Andrei during the war, a cousin he lost track of for many years, his father.

Neither the skis nor the knives are talismans. They have no magic power to animate the past. The only force that can even partially achieve that kind of magic is memory and its corollary, art. It is not surprising that eventually, in *Time and Place*, Trifonov chose to create as his protagonist neither an amateur nor a professional historian but a writer, a novelist—an artist.

VII

The Alchemy of Art

arc Chagall is the preeminent artist of upside-down houses, of topsy-turvy huts and animals, of flying lovers and skewed roofs. The truth of Chagall's art—of all art—is "crooked, fragmented, without beginning or end" (*chut' sdvinuto, chut' koso, chut' razorvano, chut' ne zakoncheno i ne nachato*). Chagall's childhood home became a primary source of his art, one to be summoned up and re-created at will. More: though the Vitebsk he knew is long gone, destroyed by time and war and progress, the Vitebsk of his canvases is indestructible.

In Trifonov's late story "A Visit to Marc Chagall," Chagall himself serves as an upside-down reflection of his old friend, Trifonov's former father-in-law, Iona Aleksandrovich. They were modernists together in the 1910s and early 1920s, and as old men they shared a tenacious thirst for life. Chagall at ninety-three had the bright eyes of his seventy-year-old self-portrait, restless curiosity, and an unquenchable love of his work. Iona Aleksandrovich was capable of both love and work until the very day of his death.

These two men led radically different lives because an accident of fate (or history) took Chagall beyond Soviet borders and left Iona Aleksandrovich at home. Chagall was the artist Trifonov's father-in-law might have become had he not been fettered by fear. In the early 1930s, when "malevolent Chagallism" (*vredonosnyi shagalizm*) was under attack, Iona Aleksandrovich yielded to the times. He tried to hide his friendship with Chagall, and he destroyed some of his own works that betrayed Chagall's influence. Even twenty years

119

later, when the word *Chagallism* still signified something "between shamanism and cabalism," he was afraid to report the theft of his most prized possession—a signed self-portrait Chagall once gave him—because it was too risky to complain.

In contrast to Chagall's exuberance and the triumph of his career, Iona Aleksandrovich led a deformed and unsatisfying artistic life. This unfulfilled painter is the counterpart (as surely he was one prototype) of Trifonov's many unfulfilled writers whose art is inextricably linked to the moral choices they make outside their art. In *Time and Place*, the last novel Trifonov wrote and prepared for publication, the hero is a novelist whose professional development is traced in careful detail and whose major work is a novel about Russian history. *Time and Place* thus forces us to attend to the particular means with which fiction specifically and art more generally interpret and animate the past, means different from those of scholarship and science. Further, the ethical dilemmas faced by characters (the hero, but not only the hero) in *Time and Place* are causally and dramatically linked with their creative work. In *Time and Place* Trifonov squarely faces the obligation the *artist*—as an artist, not just as a citizen—has toward the truth, and the consequences for his work if he shirks that obligation.

The novel appeared in print seven months after Trifonov's death. Its publication required very few revisions either by the writer's wife or by his editors. (A rumor circulated at the time that the manuscript had been held back by editors who demanded editorial changes that Trifonov was resisting, but that has never been confirmed.)[1] It is therefore tempting to treat it as the culmination of Trifonov's work, a fictional summary of Trifonov's ideas and preoccupations, his last word—no matter how much more he might have said had he lived. The novel cannot really sustain such a burden of expectation. Of Trifonov's later works, *Time and Place* is the weakest. It reiterates many of the themes, character types, and chronotopes present in *Another Life, House on the Embankment,* and *The Old Man* but lacks the structural coherence and clarity of those works. Nevertheless, because of its treatment of art and the artist's role and responsibility, *Time and Place* merits careful analysis.

Every writer that Trifonov created accepts submission and compromise, whether professional or personal, as part of his existence.

For all of them—Rebrov and Smolianov in *Long Goodbye*, Gennadii Sergeevich in *Taking Stock*, Antipov and his teacher at the Literary Institute, Boris Kiianov—those compromises have a destructive effect on the individual as artist and as man.[2] In *Time and Place* Kiianov's story is particularly revealing, both in itself and because it is the inspiration for Antipov's own novel, *Nikiforov's Syndrome*.

In 1937 Misha Teterin, Kiianov's best friend and literary collaborator, came to Kiianov's apartment. He warned him that a purge was coming, and he informed Kiianov of his own decision not to save himself at the expense of others. He gave Kiianov permission to publish their jointly written play solely under Kiianov's name, and asked that his own share of the proceeds be remitted to his wife. "Don't think I've gone crazy," he told Kiianov. "It's just that I suddenly saw clearly what's going on and what will happen. I saw the end. And I don't want to cover myself with filth before the finale like swine in a puddle" (*izmyzgat'sia, kak svin'ia v luzhe*). The finale came soon enough, complete with demands for public recantation, the denunciation of a long-gone magazine as "the worst example of ideological fellow-traveling," and the rejection of former colleagues and friends.

Teterin was arrested and spent nearly twenty years in prison, camps, and exile, while Kiianov avoided detention and spent the "same" twenty years in Moscow. In 1957, as Moscow seethes with Khrushchev's secret speech and thousands of amnestied prisoners return home, Teterin returns. It is a time when—as Anatolii Rybakov writes in *Children of the Arbat*—"thousands of people guilty of absolutely nothing were returned to life and their good names were restored to those whom it was no longer possible to return to life."[3] There is news of Teterin every day: that he has a new woman, that his wife is in despair. But he doesn't call Kiianov, indeed he seems to be avoiding him. Kiianov feels hurt. He also feels guilty.

Unlike Teterin, Kiianov played by the rules. What precisely he had to do is never stated explicitly. Whether or not he actively denounced anyone is immaterial. That he took Teterin's name off the play they coauthored, according to their agreement, but did not restore it as soon as it became possible to do so, is also immaterial. Kiianov made his choice, as the nightmare from which he wakes in a sweat signifies: his terrified dream self hides behind a column, watching the crowd passing while trying to protect himself by remaining invisible. He knows that traces of that old fear remain in him: "The old times haven't died in me . . . they're in my veins after all, in my flesh, still waiting for something" (TP 369).

Kiianov comforts himself with what are at best evasions. Not unjustifiably, he regards his old friend as an egotist of the sort familiar to us from Dostoevskii's tyrannical victims: the Underground Man, the older Marmeladovs in *Crime and Punishment*, Captain Snegirev in *Brothers Karamazov*. Former prisoners, he finds, "think that only their suffering is genuine, that the suffering of ordinary people doesn't count. It's the arrogance of unhappy people whom life has hurt, there's no bigger trap than that pride, because you don't know how to handle it. Whatever truth you might say appears out of place, whatever injustice they might perpetrate is taken as gospel" (TP 363). He argues to himself that in essence the play was his; after all, he wrote two acts and Teterin wrote only one, and that had to be rewritten substantially. He recalls how he helped Teterin's wife. "What did I do wrong?" he asks. "How am I guilty?" Yet as both his repeated soul-searching and his dreams suggest, he is consumed with guilt. He chose safety and was rewarded with survival and a fair measure of success and prosperity, but the penalty was artistic self-destruction. Conforming to one's era turns out to mean living at half strength, preserving one's prosperity from storms and tremors—"and the result," observes D. Tevekelian, "is atonement."[4] For twenty years Kiianov has not created literature; he has produced what Teterin, when they finally have their evening together, dismisses as rubbish (*barakhlo*). Teterin drunkenly continues, "I think that to write a novel like that, you didn't need to . . ." He manages to stifle the implied accusation: "you didn't need to denounce them, debase yourself, sell out."

Kiianov's comfort costs him his literary gift. His guilt costs him his life. He kills himself less because of Teterin's harsh comment about his book than because his memory of Teterin's crucial visit to him in 1937 is not corroborated by Teterin's memory. The point is not which of them is "right": Kiianov's memory may well be accurate. But Teterin does not recall the visit, or the favor he asked of Kiianov, or the agreement they reached. The whole moral justification on which Kiianov has depended for twenty years, enabling him to ignore the catty gossip of his colleagues and consider himself a man of integrity, therefore collapses. No one other than Teterin need know, but if Teterin does not recall—and Teterin genuinely does not remember—then Kiianov's image of himself as an honorable man dissolves. He has no more reason to live.

Trifonov returns to this clash of memory in two jarringly different versions of an incident in his own life. In "Short Stay in the Torture Chamber," the story meant to be part of *The Overturned House* but published belatedly, Trifonov describes a trip to the mountains near Innsbruck to cover a sports match. One of the Soviet delegates is a man he has regarded as an enemy since the anticosmopolitan campaign of 1949. At that dangerous time, when both were graduate students, the "enemy" came to Trifonov's room one evening to "warn" him: he was going to denounce Trifonov at a meeting the next day. Trifonov's memory of the conversation, and of the meeting, is crystal clear. As the two men stand together, looking down into the well of a dungeon where medieval criminals were thrown, satisfying fantasies of vengeance flood Trifonov's mind. Righteously he will accuse; rejecting his enemy's self-defense, Trifonov will throw him into the pit and no one will notice until much later.

But the enemy, when Trifonov finally confronts him, has an entirely different memory. He does not ascribe to the same behavior a different meaning; he does not justify it. He remembers something else altogether. Trifonov's "villain" stares at him in bewilderment and claims to have saved him, not destroyed him, to have prevented his expulsion from the institute. In his version Trifonov was grateful and even thanked him.

The victim surely has less reason to lacquer the past than the executioner. But Trifonov does not attempt to resolve whose memory is accurate—how could he? In "Short Stay in the Torture chamber," as in the Kiianov-Teterin conflict in *Time and Place*, his concern as a writer is rather with the process of self-preservation, the way in which memory filters out obscuring factors like jealousy in order to construct a reality that assuages guilt or shame, reassurance that one did, after all, behave honorably.

Kiianov's student, Sasha Antipov, is the only one of Trifonov's heroes who is a fiction writer. If, as has been suggested, each of Trifonov's heroes represents an alternative fate for the author himself,[5] Antipov's life suggests the most plausible variant. Not only is he a novelist, but his attitude to the past and his creative reworking

of experience into fiction simulate Trifonov's own approach. Antipov's novel, *Nikiforov's Syndrome*, is itself a tunnel stretching backward to the late eighteenth century, refracting the past in a series
of mirror images of writers who are writing novels about writers. It
is not, finally, as historian or archivist that Trifonov examines the
past, though he uses some of their tools and many of their resources;
it is as an artist, using the novelist's tools of imagination and language. If the writer "turns out to be the link in an uninterrupted
chain 'of all to all' in time and space,"[6] Antipov is Trifonov's fictional portrait of the writer at work.

The Artist as a Young Man

In *Time and Place*, Sasha Antipov's early development as a writer is
examined in the four chapters entitled "Tverskoi Boulevard," set
between February 1946 and January 1951. In each chapter Sasha
is at a different stage of personal and professional maturity, but the
chapters are linked by a clearly established relationship between art
and ethics. The everyday practical details of the writer's profession—intrigues at the Literary Institute and the Writers' Union,
writer's block, editors' advice, irregular income—are consistently
thickened by an ethical or psychological subtext. Phrases are repeated to form an incantatory index to literature's "eternal themes":
suffering, compassion, the chain of human behavior.

In the first segment Sasha is wholly preoccupied with learning to
write, which he understands only as the skillful manipulation of
words. He keeps notebooks and mentally scrutinizes everything
with an eye to its suitability as fodder for his fiction: "You had to
see that aureole [of potential re-creation] and guess its secret meaning. Not everything could be re-created, but you had to subject
everything to a momentary test" (*TP* 221).

Sasha's callow attempts to turn life, undigested, into fiction are
by turns comic and appalling, depending on the depth of the experience he is expropriating. It is funny when, for instance, he mentally weaves a story out of an incident a friend describes but is
stymied by the role of the lady in the story; alas, he knows no "la-
dies" except his sister and his cousin Tamara. It is appalling when
his mother returns from exile after the war. She recounts her ter-

rifying experience on the six-day journey from the East and tries to turn it into an amusing anecdote. So great was her hunger to see her children that she undertook the trip without the proper documentation. In her sleep she pulled the emergency cord, bringing the train to a shuddering stop. She was petrified that her guilt would be revealed by the other passengers in her car and that she would be forced to return to exile, possibly rearrested. Like Sasha Pankratov's mother in *Children of the Arbat*, or Akhmatova's women endlessly on line outside prison windows in her great poem "Requiem," or Lidiia Chukovskaia's heroine in *The Deserted House*, Sasha Antipov's mother becomes a kind of Ur-mother, a modern Mary in a twentieth-century pietà. Trifonov employs a form of narrative metonymy to portray the suffering of a generation of mothers separated from their children.

Yet Sasha himself, though moved, is more concerned with the fictional possibilities of her story than with its poignancy. His reaction is exploitative: "A story could be made out of this." He considers turning it into the story of a person returning from a German prisoner-of-war camp, in this context probably less an allusion on Trifonov's part to the impossibility, in 1946, of writing about Soviet labor camps than an insight into the young writer's attempt to "fictionalize" experience. Sasha is distressed less by his mother's pain than by the realization that his story has already been written— that all stories have already been written.[7]

For Trifonov, art was a way of coping with traumatic experience: the process of formalizing it into aesthetic patterns distanced him from the immediate pain. As a young man and a young artist, however, Trifonov probably resembled the twenty-year-old Antipov: an egotist, unable to make the emotional and imaginative leap into someone else's pain. The first night Sasha's mother is back in Moscow, she stands over his bed, sobbing silently, and asks permission to kiss the son she hasn't seen in eight years—eight years that have transformed him from a curly-haired twelve-year-old boy to a tall man in spectacles. Her longing is nearly palpable, and it tugs at his heart. At the same time, however, he considers what he might entitle the story he could write about this moment, and rejects "The Kiss" as having been used already by Chekhov.

Trifonov dissects the writer's cannibalizing of experience, and Sasha's immaturity and self-absorption, with wry tolerance. This is the chrysalis that will inevitably disintegrate if Antipov is indeed to become a writer. Thus neither malice nor condescension colors the way Trifonov presents Sasha's reaction the first time he reads aloud a story at his graduate seminar. He is elated by any word of praise and devastated by any mildly negative comment: "No one had pronounced the word 'talent.' True, neither had anyone said the words 'mediocrity,' or 'untalented,' or 'there's no hope whatever,' or 'transfer to another institute.'"

At the same time Trifonov makes sure the reader fully appreciates what his character fails to understand. The internal process by which fiction is forged out of life is far more complex, and often more painful, than the artist as a young man can possibly understand. Antipov begins to learn what literature must be about, and what a writer must attempt to do, from his teacher, Kiianov. It is Kiianov's voice that introduces the theme of "links," which Sasha pursues throughout his mature work. Kiianov tells him that actions and phrases are merely the surface of literature, below which is the substance, the "magma." He must look for the link or he will never become a writer. Until he suffers, says Kiianov, he has nothing to tell anyone else; the rest is phrase mongering. "Nothing on earth but ideas and suffering are worthy of literature," Kiianov insists.

Ironically, Sasha doesn't consider that he has genuinely suffered. "No, unfortunately he hadn't yet been forced to suffer. True, he'd lost his father ten years before, he'd had to leave Moscow ... but all that was not authentic suffering" (TP 231). His mother has become a stranger—but he "hasn't yet had to suffer"! It sounds ludicrous; it is nevertheless true. It will take years and losses and the proximity of death for him to begin to understand what he has experienced.

In the second part of "Tverskoi Boulevard," set a year later, in February 1947, Sasha begins to learn how to look below the surface for the invisible threads that explain actions and motivation. Moscow enjoys unexpectedly warm weather that February. The false spring and premature thaw are meteorological analogues of the hopes raised as the war ended: Moscow intellectuals hoped that the greater freedom of the war years would continue, and that the horrors of the 1930s would not be repeated. (One wonders what the weather actually was like that February, whether there indeed was a false spring or we are persuaded by the writer's art, as we accept

Chaucer's "drought of March" despite its total implausibility for England.) But the hopes are short-lived. A new wave of repression is under way, its poison conveyed in sighs and whispers. Sasha is vulnerable as the son of an "enemy of the people" and as a reader of the émigré writer Bunin, the grounds on which Trifonov himself was denounced during the anticosmopolitan campaign. We later learn that Kiianov was warned not to accept him into his seminar, and Kiianov himself is attacked in a newspaper article as a "covert decadent." Sasha's mother is vulnerable because she is in Moscow illegally, without a residence permit. When Sasha's angry landlord denounces her (and Sasha), only the timely intervention of a well-disposed secretary saves them.

Both as a writer and as a man, Sasha is naturally growing up in fits and starts. He is still immature enough to regard his derivative story as a chef d'oeuvre because "it has everything." (The observing persona dryly defines Sasha's "everything": descriptive passages like Paustovskii and meaningless but significant conversations like Hemingway.) Naïveté spawns humor: his sister says the story is "good but boring," and his aunt is in raptures over it ("She understood more about literature than his mother and sister. Her late husband had worked in a publishing house" [*TP* 240]).

At the same time Sasha has sufficient artistic self-confidence to reject demands to cut his story in half, remove the description of the river, remove the death of the parents, and add a trip to a construction site. "Not everything," he stubbornly insists, "can be revised."

The combination of pressures proves too much of a strain for Sasha. He falls ill, a temporary but effective way of evading what he can't cope with,[8] and recovers from his illness to a series of "firsts" in his life. The humorous sketches he sent in place of the "unrevisable" story are published. It is his first professional success, and it occurs the morning after the first time he makes love. He loses his virginity the same night as, and as a result of, witnessing a man— the friend of the girl he loves—being kicked in the head, beaten, and left to die on the street. Still correlating life and fiction in a simple equation, Sasha writes a story about the murder, but he has not yet understood Kiianov's lesson. His teacher comments: "The main thing is missing: why, really, did they punch a hole in a man? ... How did we come to live like this? Everything has its reasons,

more often than not invisible. But you have to see the chain"
(*TP* 255).

"The Chain" is the title Sasha chooses for a summer-day adven-
ture, which begins with his offering to carry a woman's bags on the
train and ends in her bed. In between he is beaten by an unknown
man on a motorcycle. He considers and rejects possible explanations
suitable for a story, the "reasons" Kiianov urges him to find. None
is as wild as the real explanation: the woman's brother has a passion
for justice that takes the form of beating up people who violate his
standards of courtesy or don't stop behaving "rudely" when he tells
them to. His apology is equally implausible: he asks Sasha to take a
swing at him, "to even things up, to be fair."

The last part of Sasha's apprenticeship as a writer resumes after
the interruption of two chapters narrated by the *I*. It is again 1947,
spring and summertime, again "Tverskoi Boulevard." Sasha continues to amass material for his fiction. He travels to the Kuban where
he hopes to find Natasha, the girl he loved, who ran away from
Moscow after her friend was killed. Meanwhile he fills his notebooks
with folk idioms, local names and curses, proverbs and adages.[9] He
collects them all, as he collects the experience of smoking *makhra*,
a coarse tobacco, and drinking moonshine. He cold-bloodedly "collects" Iakim, a war hero who has lost his sight, and Iakim's wife and
children.

Sasha can't get over his magnificent piece of luck in stumbling
upon such a ready-made fictional hero: "Heroism, self-sacrifice, suffering and loneliness—what could be better [*blagodatnei*] for prose!"
Iakim seems to him a real-life Platon Karataev who captures and
articulates deep truths in simple language: fascism, for instance,
means "lawlessness, and the worst people coming to the fore."

Iakim leads Sasha to Natasha, whom he has given up looking for.
Eager to show off to Natasha his professional success and his sexual
maturity, Sasha is indifferent to Iakim's fear that he will take Natasha away from the farm. But his joy at finding Natasha and making
love to her is short-lived: he loves her, he cannot help her, they
have to separate. He begins to understand Iakim's suffering only
when he himself is in pain. Suddenly the words of Natasha's great-
grandmother's song become more than an example of uncorrupted
ethnomusicology. The folk idioms he has been writing down as an

intellectual exercise become poignant expressions of emotions he
himself feels:

> And I saddle my steed, go out of the yard.
> Run, my steed, run, my little raven, to the still Dunai.
> There I will dismount and I will think,
> Whether to choke myself, or drown myself,
> Or turn back and go home . . . (TP 317)

> *A ia konika sedlaiu, so dvorika vyezzhaiu.*
> *Bezhi, moi konik, bezhi, moi voronik, do tikhogo Dunaiu.*
> *Tam ia vstanu, podumaiu:*
> *ili mne dushit'sia, ili utopit'sia,*
> *ili do domu vorotit'sia . . .*

The final segment of "Tverskoi Boulevard" begins in triumph
that turns sour almost immediately. Sasha has signed his first contract and received his first advance, with which he treats his friends
Miron and Kvashin to a meal. But it is 1950 and an ugly public
mood darkens their private celebration. Miron quarrels with Kvashin,
who has written a book review "to order," praising a book generally
agreed to be contemptible. The brash young men at a neighboring
table direct a round of petty but patently anti-Semitic jeers and
taunts at Miron; it escalates into a fistfight out on the street. Both
the anti-Semitism and Kvashin's book review are signs of the times.
So is the disappearance of the editor who signed Sasha's contract.
When Sasha offers to wait in his office until he returns, he is told
flatly that the editor will not be returning. There is a new editor, a
man named Saiasov.

Sasha is drawn into a plagiarism case that is part and parcel of
the atmosphere of the early 1950s. He is asked to testify at a trial,
to give his professional opinion on whether a writer named Dvoinikov has plagiarized a text. Since he is only a graduate student, it
is clear that the lawyer who asked him (Miron's father, in fact) hopes
that Sasha will be flattered and will reciprocate by supporting his
client. Saiasov, the editor who now has the power to publish Sasha's
manuscript, is involved in the case, for his brother is one of those
making the accusations against Dvoinikov. Saiasov calls Dvoinikov
a "half-baked intellectual," a "protector of people of dubious reputation," poisonous rhetoric typical of those years.

Saiasov's and his ally Priakhin's affability barely masks their viciousness. Priakhin's amiable concern gives way to menacing allusions to Sasha's mother's precarious professional situation. Even worse, he addresses his remarks not to Sasha, who might challenge him, but to Sasha's far more timid sister. Saiasov blackmails Sasha's future wife, Tania: unless she sleeps with him, he will denounce her father, a former prisoner. She yields.

The plagiarism case is a tangle of corruption. Everyone involved tries either to bribe Sasha (with money or promises of publication) or to blackmail him emotionally. After twisting and turning to find a way out, after actually backing out temporarily, Sasha realizes he has no choice. "Since there was no way of getting out of it, and nothing to regret, and being a coward didn't suit him, there was only one way out—to learn the truth" (TP 347).

The truth is that Dvoinikov is a mixture of contradictory qualities. (His name, "double," suggests his dual nature, just as the name Antipov suggests opposition, contrast.) He did sign his name to work which, gray and mediocre though it was, he had not written. At the same time he used his position to offer generous help to people in difficulties (implicitly, political difficulties). He had a mistress, yet he loved his wife; he was bold about some matters and craven about others.

Sasha testifies that he finds no plagiarism in the texts in question. In doing so, he defends that part of Dvoinikov which was willing to take the risk of helping people, the risk of behaving generously and with courage, and he emulates that generosity and courage. Much as the I's emulation of Antipov's behavior during the war is a positive corroboration of its underlying values, so Antipov's defense of Dvoinikov affirms the qualities Dvoinikov has demonstrated. In the long run his integrity is rewarded—by Tania's love and Kiianov's help in getting his book published. But because he acts without calculation of such returns, which are unforeseeable, and because the immediate consequences for him are negative, his courage is not compromised.

"Tverskoi Boulevard IV" ends with Kiianov's offer to take a look at Antipov's manuscript. It is an appropriate ending to four chapters that detail Sasha's formative years as a writer, his development from tyro to incipient professional. Moreover, although Kiianov has nothing at all to do with the Dvoinikov case, he is—like Dvoinikov—a mass of contradictions, a complex mixture of cowardice and daring, timidity and impetuosity. As Dvoinikov is mirrored in Kiianov, so is Kiianov—with his "unfulfilled life"—mirrored in Antipov's hero, Nikiforov, and in Antipov himself.

The Unfulfilled Novelist

As an artistic device, *Nikiforov's Syndrome* does not work very well. It draws attention to itself as a device at the expense of its substance, thus it obscures rather than clarifies Trifonov's view of the relationship between the past and the present. The doubling principle of *Time and Place*, which finds expression in its narrative voices as well as in several minor characters,[10] becomes excessive in this novel within a novel. Moreover, *Nikiforov's Syndrome* is excessively self-referential. When Sasha sends his manuscript out, the readers' reactions paraphrase (and preview) some of the criticism directed against Trifonov's own work. Writing a novel about a writer is criticized as a subject of last resort for authors who have nothing left to say; Sasha is accused of neglecting the "social roots" of his hero's "disease" and the life of the nation against which the hero's actions are played out.[11]

Its failures notwithstanding, *Nikiforov's Syndrome* offers a glimpse of the writer's laboratory—his own reactions to his prose (as well as the routine of writing) and what he does with the *realia* of life as it penetrates his fiction. Like Trifonov himself, Antipov as a mature writer no longer attempts to cannibalize immediate experience. He has learned that experience, like a yeast dough, requires both time and imagination to be ready for manipulation into fiction, and that understanding only comes retrospectively. Thus, while he is emotionally engrossed in, even obsessed with, his love affair with the beautiful filmmaker Irina, the affair does not get into the pages of his manuscript. Instead it interrupts them, in contextually irrelevant phrases and sentences which Trifonov separates by the use of italics. Writing is an uninterrupted process; "it does not stop because of external events but takes in and absorbs them, constantly reconsidering and comparing them, searching for the thread."[12]

Antipov works on his novel as his twenty-year marriage to Tania unravels. His affair with Irina is neither the cause nor the effect of that unraveling. Indeed, the "reasons" offered for the disintegration of their marriage—Tania's reluctance to go out, her asociability, Sasha's restlessness—are symptoms of that disintegration rather than actual causes. This estrangement is no one's fault. The culprit, if there is one, is time, which separates them, so that—as Teterin explained to Antipov about himself and Kiianov—the ice floes on which they stand drift in different directions.[13]

The affair is partly an answer to the need every Trifonov hero experiences for the possibility of "another life." The thought of "changing destiny" grips them, offering them comfort.[14] These crises seem to run in twenty-year cycles, a result of the fact that most of Trifonov's male heroes have been married about twenty years when they reach their troubled mid-forties. The narrator of *Taking Stock*, ensconced in the Central Asian village to which he has temporarily fled, uses the same measure in thinking about his unhappy marriage:

> We should not have lived together for twenty years.... Twenty years is no joke! In twenty years forests thin out and the soil becomes depleted. Even the best house requires repair. Turbines stop functioning. And as for the tremendous advances made by science in twenty years— it's awesome to contemplate! Revolutionary discoveries take place in all areas of human knowledge. Whole cities are rebuilt.... Twenty years! A time span which can destroy all hopes. (*TS* 123)

Sasha's affair with Irina begins in the summer of 1971, when they meet on a trip to Eastern Europe, and continues throughout the fall and into the spring. He is writing *Nikiforov's Syndrome* all the while, or rather he is rewriting, trying to get it to work. Nikiforov's "syndrome" consists of a fear of life, "more accurately, fear of the realities of life," and a desire to avoid looking at things squarely. It is a disease that afflicts several characters in *Time and Place*, including Sasha himself in the following chapter. Sasha claims that Nikiforov is modeled after Kiianov and that he has given to Nikiforov only the detritus or trivia (*sor*) of his own life, as if the detritus of life was distinct from, and contradicted, its significance. In fact, meaning arises only thanks to the existence and in the context of the detritus.

Sasha confutes his own claim by distinguishing the novel from the "hackwork" (*khalturshchina*) that pays the bills: "Writing 'Syn-

drome' was an entirely different matter. It was as if he were operating on himself. At times it was painful" (*TP* 404). It is a process
of self-examination, like Olga's purifying search for her own con-
tribution to Sergei's unhappiness in *Another Life*, and like Letunov's
exhumation of the past in *The Old Man*, stripping layers of bloody
bandages off a wound. In the words of A. Mikhailov, "Operating
on oneself requires courage and the acceptance of pain and suffering, but it is the essential condition for self-knowledge."[15]

Each of the anguished authors within *Nikiforov's Syndrome* tries to
understand the mysterious death of his "hero." The first author is
Klembovskii, described as a "wild man" or "madcap" (*sumasbrod*) of
the 1840s. He is tormented by having informed on his friends, and
his writing is his only means of coping with his guilt. He invents as
his hero a Russian Voltairist of the 1780s. Klembovskii is himself
the creation of one Syromiatnikov, who dies from drink, and he in
turn is created by Vsevolodov, a dreamer, poet, and terrorist who
returns from exile in England for the 1917 revolution. Vsevolodov
is killed in the Urals during the Civil War under "mysterious circumstances." Nikiforov, who supposedly met him in 1918 in Iaro-
slavl before a White uprising, in fact creates him, as Sasha creates
Nikiforov—and, of course, as Trifonov creates Sasha.

No historic incident connected with any of these characters is
presented in the novel, though each era evokes historical associations for a knowledgeable reader. Instead, this spiral of men creates
an outline of the history of the Russian intelligentsia, the most salient and consistent characteristic of which was its stance vis-à-vis
official authority. Each "author" and each "hero" is defined either
directly or by implication in terms of his relationship to the state.
The eighteenth-century Voltairist, Ryndich, is a member of a secret
and illegal society, the Masonic Brotherhood. His creator, Klembovskii, collaborated with the secret police. *His* creator, Syromiatnikov, is one of the *raznochintsy*, well-educated but socially and
professionally stymied young men of the mid-nineteenth century
whose most famous fictional representative is Turgenev's Bazarov.
Son of a deacon and a journalist for the monthly *Sovremennik*, Syromiatnikov is almost by definition an oppositionist. His author is a
revolutionary exiled to Arkhangelsk for his terrorist acts. The list
culminates in the somewhat sorry figure of Nikiforov, the weak So-

viet *intelligent* of the Stalinist and post-Stalin years whose survival
in those dreadful years largely depends on his wife, Goga, and her
highly placed lover.

Sasha writes at length about Goga and her "innocent betrayals,"
which may not have been betrayals at all, since they served to save
her husband. Without transition we hear the writer commenting on
his own work: "Now that's good. That's getting near the truth.
None of us knows whose hand—not necessarily hand, it might be
someone's back or chest, it might be someone's outstretched foot—
protects us from misfortune." (He does not consciously recall, but
the reader remembers the institute secretary in 1950 who tore up
the denunciation against Sasha.) Sasha only gradually understands
that part of Nikiforov's syndrome stems from a fear of losing Goga.

The fear of losing Goga keeps Nikiforov blind to her infidelity.
When her first husband turns up and appeals to her to use her connections—that is, her lover—to help him, Nikiforov can't understand what "connections" Goga might have: "He saw everything
clearly and saw absolutely nothing, the secret mechanism of fear
clouded his vision like cataracts" (*TP* 421). He fears that if Goga
should leave him by choice, and not by some unforeseeable and
inescapable act of fate, it would destroy him.

All creators of fiction—Trifonov, Antipov, and Nikiforov alike—
take the raw material for their work from life. Goga's first husband
once wrote out ten "rules" of wifely behavior, which Nikiforov
wants to use in his work; we later learn that Sasha has taken those
rules from a man who is courting his mother and has given them
to his novel. (Who knows where Trifonov got them from?) Sasha's
affair with Irina has no explicit parallel in Nikiforov's life, but it is
a source of emotional truth for Sasha's fiction. He can portray Nikiforov's jealousy based on firsthand knowledge; he exploits Irina
just as Nikiforov exploits Goga when he asks her to write down her
reactions to the death of an old lover so that he can "use" them.

The process of turning life into fiction is more complex than the
young Sasha thought, and more complex than nonwriters think.
The doctor who agreed to perform the abortion on Tania in 1953
was eager for Sasha to write up his life, which was full of "interesting
stories." Twenty-five years later, the book dealer Markusha is
equally sure that his amatory and other experiences are the stuff of
best-selling literature. It takes Antipov—as, one must assume, it

took Trifonov—many years to understand that literature doesn't grow out of other people's adventures, unless those adventures touch something within the writer himself. For that matter, literature doesn't grow even out of the author's own experiences, unless and until he understands them. Without that he has nothing to say.

When he rereads *Nikiforov's Syndrome*, which has been rejected by his editors, Sasha realizes that he has failed. Months later, after many reworkings and after his affair with Irina has ended, he explains to his mother that the requisite "digging," without which the book simply would not work, was beyond him. And yet he is equally unable to let go of it because it is the only book that really matters to him.

In a sense Sasha's failure explains both the ethical and aesthetic relationship of Trifonov's first book, *Students*, to *House on the Embankment*, his "rewriting" of *Students* some twenty-five years later. As a writer working within a specific milieu with specific historical roots and circumstances, Trifonov felt a sense of responsibility toward his readers to get as close as possible to what he perceived to be true about that world. What he understood in 1975 was not the same as what he had understood in 1950, just as what Antipov understands—about reality and about literature—changes over the thirty years we "know" him.

The many parallels between the two works are clearly meant to force a comparison and to alert the reader to the ways in which the two books differ.[16] The name of *Students'* hero, Vadim Belov, is transformed into its virtual anagram, Vadim Glebov. The central conflict—between the prevailing politico-literary dogma and the professor who comes under attack—is identical; identical too are its time and place. Trifonov's distaste for *Students* did not come only from shame at having written a conformist work which reflected the meretricious standards that prevailed at the time. If that were all, *House on the Embankment* would simply invert *Students*, with disapproval replacing approbation and positive heroes transformed into villains.[17] Through his manipulation of authorial voice, Trifonov certainly weighs Glebov, and equally certainly finds him wanting. But as much as he rejects Glebov's behavior, he also rejects the authorial complacency of *Students*—the categorical certainty that found moral labels and aesthetic clichés attractive, and the era that "dictated cruelty of judgment and demanded . . . above all passing sentence."[18] In its stead he substitutes a more complicated and artistically subtle depiction of the Glebovs of Soviet society.[19]

The issue of responsibility for one's earlier work is addressed directly in Trifonov's late story "Cats or Hares?" which was published posthumously. The writer returns to a town in Italy he had visited twenty years earlier and had described in the 1964 story "Memory of Genzano." To his distress he learns that the proprietor of a restaurant he recalls fondly was accused of passing off roasted cat as roasted hare. Should he rewrite the story, he wonders? Is the earlier story false, invalidated by this new information that exposes as fraudulent the experience on which the story was based?

Trifonov concludes that, on the one hand, the sensation of happiness he felt then was real, not illusory; it was genuine, not false. On the other hand, had he known about the cats at the time, he would have had an obligation to say so: "There are poor roasted cats everywhere, and a writer does not have the right to pretend that they aren't. He is obliged to expose them, however deeply or slyly they are hiding." Explicitly identifying the artist's obligation to the truth, Trifonov implicitly suggests that his own younger self did not grasp the realities he was attempting to deal with in his art. His happiness eighteen years earlier was genuine. To deny its reality by exposing its meretricious underpinnings is a distorting application of hindsight. His hero Antipov had once refused to revise his story, arguing that "not everything can be revised." Trifonov declines as well: "One cannot correct that which is not subject to correction, inaccessible to touch—that which flows through us" (CH 59).

We never learn if Antipov finishes *Nikiforov's Syndrome*, though everything suggests that he does not. In the novel's penultimate chapter Antipov's isolation from all that is meaningful in life is a sign of his psychological ill health. No healthy Trifonov character ever stands alone, and no healthy individual abdicates on the multitude of choices—from apartment furniture to love affairs—that confront him. As Antipov suffers the acute pain of a coronary he thinks of his mother's words, "Everything has its time and its place." He realizes that a man can only try to live worthily in that place and time he is given.[20] In the final analysis, one cannot avoid either one's fate or one's self.

Conclusion

Iurii Trifonov died in 1981. Since the latter half of that decade
the Soviet Union has been involved in a process that is profoundly affecting its economic, social, and political structures, and
has already transformed its cultural consciousness. The effect of
glasnost' on the distribution of cultural products has made available
to Soviet readers a host of literary works. The few texts Trifonov
was unable to publish during his lifetime were among the first fruits
of *glasnost'*, appearing in print in the autumn of 1986, when the
incipient and fragile relaxation of censorship was still greeted with
wary astonishment.

A more fundamental and far-reaching effect of *glasnost'* is the
disappearance of fear in the Soviet Union. Soviet citizens are no
longer afraid to say what they think. Soviet writers are no longer
cribbed and cramped by the apprehension that once inevitably ac-
companied any attempt or intent to publish through official channels. They can tackle head-on where once they had to sidle; they
can spell out where once they had to hint. The absence of fear and
the possibility of directness are exhilarating.

The works of fiction that ushered in *glasnost'*—many of them
novels written years earlier, like Rybakov's *Children of the Arbat*, Dudintsev's *White Robes*, and Granin's *The Bison*—took full advantage
of the opportunity to be explicit. "Ideological blockbusters," they
are all, to one degree or another, fictionalized exposés, publicistic
statements within the literary framework of socialist realism. Whatever their artistic shortcomings, they are, in Helena Goscilo's words,

"praiseworthy in their moral fervor and their probity from the standpoint of refurbished liberal ideology,"[1] and they have been of immense importance in the metamorphosis of Soviet society.

Yet directness is not exclusively advantageous in literature. Ellipsis, the mask of metaphor, and the obliquity of narrative disguise can also serve the ends of artistry. This is not said in praise of censorship. It is false reasoning that offers the greatness of Russian literature, always produced in conditions of censorship, as proof that censorship is beneficial to literature. What *can* be argued is that writers evolve strategies to deal with specific circumstances and exigencies, and that those strategies may be artistically successful. The same writers would have responded to other circumstances—the absence of censorship, for instance—in other, perhaps no less satisfying, ways.

The constraints and consequent self-censorship that plagued all "official" Soviet writers in the late 1960s and 1970s did not prevent Trifonov from using his art to explore certain controversial subjects and ideas. On the contrary, it was precisely his artistry that allowed him to address those subjects. He never filled in the blank spots explicitly, but he did so indirectly via structural juxtaposition and narrative masks. He evolved a literary style that, despite the existence of censorship, permitted oblique examination of what have come to resemble public obsessions in the explosion of information and analysis characteristic of *glasnost'*.

Those obsessions have specifically to do with the facts of Soviet history and the psychological processes that generated and in part explain them. If, as Dmitri Likhachev says, memory is "the conscience of a nation," what *glasnost'* has achieved is a reactivation of memory and conscience—individual, societal, and institutional—in the Soviet Union. Trifonov's fiction anticipated that reanimation and was one of the relatively few signs that such a process was going on under the frozen surface of official life. At a time when memory was largely shrouded and falsification was still the norm, Trifonov pushed aside the veils and, albeit gingerly, abjured the lies.

Trifonov's historical imagination was limited to a specific intellectual and political tradition, and his main characters are almost all members of that tradition. His fiction is mute about many of the phases of Soviet savagery: the purges of Socialist Revolutionaries and Mensheviks in the 1920s, for example, and the bloodletting of collectivization. He was and continues to be reproached by émigré and Soviet critics for doing so. Yet consciousness can only be a product of individual experience, either personally or imaginatively perceived. Of the encompassing violence that has constituted a large part of Soviet history, Trifonov was able to penetrate imaginatively and therefore convey to his readers what touched him and his family most directly: the Great Terror that took his father, and his private baptism by fire, the anticosmopolitan campaign.

Trifonov's failure to mention (let alone imprecate) the destruction of the peasantry and other atrocities must be noted. It need not, however, be construed as signifying personal indifference; nor does it undermine the validity of his art. As a novelist, he found the grist for his fiction in the experiences of the revolutionary intelligentsia, who were responsible for creating a state that eventually destroyed them, and their children, who reaped the whirlwind.[2] For Trifonov's father and men like him, neither the suppression of the Socialist Revolutionaries in the early 1920s nor the enforced starvation of collectivization shook their faith in Bolshevism. Whatever their disagreements with Stalin's policies, they rationalized those disagreements and came to terms with those policies. Not until the Great Terror did they open their eyes. For better or worse, *their* year of revelation was 1937. Only then did they recognize the end of what *their* revolution had been fought for.

Certain facts could not be stated plainly. Trifonov could only assume them to be knowledge shared by himself and his readers and trust in the readiness of those readers to understand allusions. In lieu of explicit description of those facts, Trifonov attempted to explain what generated them and what ensued from them. Deeply concerned with understanding the transformation and perversion of the Soviet state under Stalin, Trifonov understood that one man alone could not create such a deformation. It required the passive acceptance, if not active support, of major segments of society, and particularly of its powerful elite. He therefore tried repeatedly to examine the psychological processes that allowed men like his father—men admirable in many ways—to practice what amounted to a form of doublethink and to persuade themselves that what was happening around them, in part due to their own actions and decisions, was logically explicable, or was a series of isolated errors, or was not happening at all.

Trifonov never justified this doublethink, and he suggested that its consequences are devastating. Nevertheless, he was less concerned with judgment than with comprehension. He therefore recreated the process of denial in all his fiction, varying only the contexts and specific details, to force his readers to understand how it could have happened, indeed how it did happen, how it could, perhaps, happen still.

When he portrayed that phenomenon of denial and traced its ideological and historical roots among Old Bolsheviks of his father's generation, he wrote with immense sadness and love. To the mistakes they made, Trifonov juxtaposed and to some degree counterposed their hopes and the beauty of their ideals. They had at least a vision of egalitarianism and justice, however they ultimately compromised it by their own actions. In his fiction, even the worst of them—the most misguided and self-deluding, those unconsciously pretending to a purity of principle that camouflaged darker motives—are not covetous of personal material gain, or intentionally unscrupulous.

Trifonov was harsher when he portrayed denial and corruption in his own generation. Most of the men of his generation lack even comprehension of, let alone sympathy for or belief in, ideals beyond their personal prosperity or success. The few who retain such ideals, even in a diluted version, are misunderstood and even reviled by their society, which has no room for such dreamers.

To be sure, Trifonov's generation were the children orphaned by 1937; they came of age between 1946 and 1953. As such, they were victims. But more often than not, Trifonov portrayed them as victims who came to participate in the system that victimized them and to share in the venality that displaced their fathers' vision. They became collaborators with a system that destroyed moral values.

The style of Trifonov's mature prose enabled him to examine these moral dilemmas without trespassing onto clearly forbidden territory and thereby precluding publication. By placing the present back-to-back with the past, he produced a collision analogous to the dramatic montage of film and almost forced his readers to infer the significance of their interrelationship. He created the opportunity for readers to infer or apprehend the "threads," the "chain" in human behavior that he himself believed to exist. Loath to comment directly on the integrity or corruption of his characters, he

chose circuity instead. His judgments were derived from an accu-
mulation of clues: the opinions of other characters, the replication
of experience, and linguistic patterns. Trifonov manipulated narrative voice in order to penetrate a character's thoughts and thereby
enlist reader sympathy, yet he contextualized those thoughts so
that the character's own evaluation, often defensive or exculpatory,
is far from the last word.

Trifonov's time montages, narrative interplay, and polysemous
symbols never modified the essential realism (hence accessibility)
of his prose. They became far more than a means of outwitting dull
censors. They served to elaborate the complex grids of time and
place, fate and choice, experience and reflection, that he believed
to be the matrices of individual and societal life. He chose the means
uniquely available to him as an artist to discharge his responsibility
toward the past and articulate what he perceived to be the truth.

In the Soviet Union today, even after several years of glasnost',
there is a fierce hunger to understand where Russia went wrong and
who was responsible. It encompasses serious scholarly inquiry and
imaginative work, as well as an often crude search for scapegoats.
Increasingly, historians trace the origins of the Stalinist terror specifically to Leninist principles and policies, in some cases proceeding
to a flat rejection of Bolshevism and Leninism in toto and to a sometimes simplified analysis of alternatives to the Bolsheviks.

Trifonov himself never rejected the ideals of the October Revolution. Rather, he came to understand that the Bolsheviks, blurring
ends and means in their quest for power, were in large measure
responsible for the destruction of those ideals. In the years before
glasnost' unlocked the Pandora's box of the Bolshevik legacy, Trifonov's fiction was unique in the official press for its attempt to
settle accounts with the "revolutionary impatience" of his father's
generation, "at once the curse and high note" of his own. It was a
process that gave him enormous pain.[3]

The younger generation of writers, especially the more innova-
tive and imaginative writers, by and large lacks both the bond and
the pain. The most gifted of the writers who have come to prominence in the era of glasnost' (Liudmila Petrushevskaia, Mikhail Ku-
raev, Tatiana Tolstaia, and Vladimir Makanin, to mention a few),
posit a universe that derives little meaning and few values from the
Soviet past. Every kind of idealization—let alone sentimentality—

is absent from their work, as indeed is certainty of any sort. As a result, their work is more often farcical than tragic; they turn away from realism—as if with distaste or recognizing its hopeless inadequacy—toward fantasy and grotesquerie.

Yet some, at least, of Trifonov's questions are theirs as well. They too ask if history has meaning in itself or is merely another form of fiction. They too wonder about the artist's responsibility to the past. They too resist articulating an authoritative or monologic authorial stance, reject the prophetic voice, and "dialogize or obscure even tentatively implied values and hierarchies" in favor of a partnership with the reader.[4]

Trifonov's fiction was readily available to these younger writers during the years of their creative maturation. In the ongoing dialogue that artists conduct with their progenitors, he is one of their chief collocutors. They and their readers have already exploited the welcome disappearance of censorship by experimenting in every direction, aesthetically as well as politically, and they will continue to do so. Yet we must also penetrate the paradox of good literature created in conditions of censorship. That is the paradox of the great Russian literature of the nineteenth century, and that is the paradox of Iurii Trifonov's art.

Notes

The following editions were used for quotations from the Trifonov texts discussed in this book: *Another Life and House on the Embankment*, trans. Michael Glenny (New York: Simon and Schuster, 1983); abbreviated in the text, respectively, as *AL* and *HE*; translations have been modified where necessary. *The Old Man*, trans. Jacqueline Edwards and Mitchell Schneider (New York: Simon and Schuster, 1984); abbreviated in the text as *OM*; translations have been modified when necessary. *Time and Place* (*Vremia i mesto*), in *Vechnyè temy* (Moscow: Sovetskii pisatel', 1985); translations mine; abbreviated in the text as *TP*. *The Disappearance* (*Ischeznovenie*), *Druzhba narodov* 1 (January 1987): 6–94; translations mine (an English translation by David Lowe is forthcoming from Ardis); abbreviated in the text as *D*. *The Exchange* (trans. E. Proffer), *The Long Goodbye*, and *Taking Stock* (trans. H. Burlingame), were printed together as *The Long Goodbye* (Ann Arbor, Mich.: Ardis, 1979) and are abbreviated as *E*, *LG*, and *TS*, respectively; translations have been modified where necessary. Citations from the stories comprising *The Overturned House* are taken from *Novyi mir* (July 1981): 58–87; translations mine. All translations from Russian are mine unless noted otherwise.

Introduction

1. Vera Dunham, *In Stalin's Time: Middleclass Values in Soviet Fiction* (Cambridge: Cambridge University Press, 1976), x. Dunham's book is an outstanding example of a quasi-literary, quasi-sociological analysis for which such fiction is supremely appropriate.

2. The literature on this subject is voluminous. Among the best on

the early period are Rufus Mathewson's *The Positive Hero in Russian Literature* (Stanford: Stanford University Press, 1984); Abbot Gleason, ed., *Bolshevik Culture: Experiment and Order in the Russian Revolution* (Bloomington: Indiana University Press, 1989); Robert Maguire, *Red Virgin Soil: Soviet Literature in the 1920s* (Princeton: Princeton University Press, 1968). For the 1930s and 1940s, see Katerina Clark, *The Soviet Novel: History as Ritual* (Chicago: University of Chicago Press, 1981); and Dunham, *In Stalin's Time*; for 1946–53, see Walter Vickery, *Cult of Optimism* (Bloomington: Indiana University Press, 1963).

3. Vladimir Nabokov, "Russian Writers, Censors, and Readers," in *Lectures on Russian Literature* (New York: Harcourt Brace Jovanovich, 1981), 2–3.

4. Of the many descriptions *cum* definitions of socialist realism, Vladimir Voinovich's is perhaps the most apt: "Socialist realism is praise of the leaders in terms they can understand" (cited by John Garrard and Carol Garrard, *Inside the Soviet Writers' Union* [New York: Free Press, 1990], 169).

5. See Mathewson, *The Positive Hero*, 211–32; Garrard and Garrard, *Inside the Soviet Writers' Union*, 15–43.

6. Garrard and Garrard, *Inside the Soviet Writers' Union*, 81.

7. Ronald Hingley, *Russian Writers and Soviet Society 1917–1978* (New York: Random House, 1979), 49.

8. Aleksandr Solzhenitsyn, Letter to the Fourth Congress of Soviet Writers, in *In Quest of Justice*, ed. A. Brumberg (New York: Praeger, 1970), 245–47.

9. For the tightening alignment of the Writers' Union with the party, see Garrard and Garrard, *Inside the Soviet Writers' Union*, 80–105.

10. Hingley, *Russian Writers*, 227.

11. For fuller descriptions of incentives and disincentives see Hingley, *Russian Writers*, 196–97; and Garrard and Garrard, *Inside the Soviet Writers' Union*, 122–36.

12. See Natalia Il'ina's exposé of corruption in the literary bureaucracy, "Welcome, Young and Unknown Tribe ... ," *Ogonek* 2 (1988): 23–26.

13. Garrard and Garrard, who outline these steps (*Inside the Soviet Writers' Union*, 123–24), add two which would rarely—though occasionally—have applied to literary texts: the KGB and the Propaganda Department of the Party Central Committee. Lev Loseff arranges the steps in a sequence beginning with self-censorship, through public discussion and editorial censorship, to state ideological, administrative, and finally party censorship. See Loseff, *The Beneficence of Censorship* (Munich: Verlag Otto Sagner, 1984), app. 1, 232–34.

14. Martin Dewhirst and Robert Farrell, eds., *The Soviet Censorship* (Metuchen, N.J.: Scarecrow Press, 1973), contains a sensitive explanation of how the function of editor overlaps with that of censor. See especially pp. 50–95.

15. Anatolii Gladilin, *The Making and Unmaking of a Soviet Writer* (Ann Arbor, Mich.: Ardis, 1979), 45.

16. V. Arkhipov's 1968 review of James Billington's *The Icon and the Axe*, for instance, cites Billington's often unflattering assessments of Lenin's commitment to truth and morality. See Loseff, *Beneficence of Censorship*, 109–10.

17. See Josephine Woll and Vladimir Treml, *Soviet Dissident Literature: A Critical Guide* (Boston: G. K. Hall, 1983).

18. Hingley, *Russian Writers*, 163.

19. See Kathleen Parthé, *The Radiant Past: Russian Village Prose from Ovechkin to Rasputin*, forthcoming from Princeton University Press (1991).

20. Andrei Siniavskii, "Samizdat and the Rebirth of Literature," *Index on Censorship* 9.4 (August 1980): 9.

21. For an analysis of Liubimov's work from 1964 to 1984, see Aleksandr Gershkovich, *Theater on the Taganka (Teatr na Taganke)* (Benson, Vt.: Chalidze Publications, 1986).

22. Loseff, *Beneficence of Censorship*, 110.

23. Ibid., 58.

24. Ibid., 219.

25. That is true in the paradigmatic "thaw" novel, Erenburg's *Thaw*, and much more so in later stories by, for instance, Natalia Baranskaia and Irina Velembovskaia.

26. See Jack V. Haney, "The Revival of Interest in the Russian Past in the Soviet Union," *Slavic Review* 32.1 (March 1973): 1–16, and two commentaries in the same issue: Thomas E. Bird, "New Interest in Old Russian Things: Literary Ferment, Religious Perspectives, and National Self-Assertion" (17–28), and George L. Kline, "Religion, National Character and the 'Rediscovery of Russian Roots'" (29–40).

27. One of the best short analyses of village prose can be found in Geoffrey Hosking, *Beyond Socialist Realism* (London: Granada, 1980), 50–83.

28. Katerina Clark analyzes how one such text yields meanings acceptable to orthodox critics but can also be read in a variety of other ways. See Clark, "The Mutability of the Canon: Socialist Realism and Chingiz Aitmatov's *I dol'she veka dlitsia den'*," *Slavic Review* 43.4 (1984): 573–87.

29. Igor Zolotusskii, "The Ennobling Word" (*Vozvyshaiushchee slovo*), *Literaturnoe obozrenie* (July 1988): 16.

30. Viktor Toporov, "The Phenomenon of Disappearance" (*Fenomen ischeznoveniia*), *Literaturnoe obozrenie* (January 1988): 23.

31. Craig Whitney, "Russian Writer, Not a Dissident, Critic of Society," *New York Times*, 24 October 1977.

32. Toporov, "Phenomenon of Disappearance," 24.

I   Preparations

1. He had already published one sketch, "Broad Compass: A Feuilleton" (*Shirokaia diapazon: Fel'eton*), in *Moskovskii Komsomolets*, 12 April 1947.

2. Trifonov, "Notes of a Neighbor" (*Zapiski soseda*) [1973], in *Izbrannye proizvedeniia*, 2 vols. (Moscow: Khudozhestvennaia literatura, 1978), 2:522.

3. Dunham, *In Stalin's Time*, 46.

4. Walter Vickery, "Zhdanovism (1946–1963)," in *Literature and Revolution in Soviet Russia 1917–62*, ed. Max Hayward and Leopold Labedz (New York: Oxford University Press, 1963), 99.

5. See Mathewson, *The Positive Hero*, for a general analysis of the paradigm of the positive hero. For the specific period of 1946–53, see Vickery, *Cult of Optimism*; and Clark, *The Soviet Novel*, 191–209.

6. Natalia Ivanova, *The Prose of Iurii Trifonov* (*Proza Iuriia Trifonova*) (Moscow: Sovetskii pisatel', 1984), 17.

7. Dunham, *In Stalin's Time*, 206.

8. Trifonov, *Studenty, Novyi mir* (November 1950): 89.

9. Evgenii Shklovskii, "Phenomenon of Life" (*Fenomen zhizni*), *Literaturnoe obozrenie* (April 1986): 66.

10. Ivanova, *The Prose of Iurii Trifonov*, 38–39.

11. Referring to their experience of the Stalinist terror and the arrests of their parents, Craig Whitney compared Trifonov to Bulat Okudzhava, Vasilii Aksenov, and other "official" writers: "Only their eloquence makes them different from millions of their countrymen" ("USSR—The Legacy of Stalin," *New York Times*, 16 December 1979). Aksenov subsequently became involved in publishing the independent literary almanac *Metropol*; those activities and the publication abroad of his novel *The Burn* shifted him into the "unofficial" category and forced his emigration in 1980.

12. Ivanova, *The Prose of Iurii Trifonov*, 92.

13. Each of the works mentioned circulated in *samizdat* and was published in the West in the late 1960s. Nekrich's book *was* published in the Soviet Union in 1965 but became unavailable within a year: it was removed from library shelves and bookstores.

14. Tatiana Patera argues that the end of the story reflects the gloom of liberals after the Siniavskii-Daniel trial of 1966, and that the repressive

climate of 1966 precluded publication. By 1968, when it finally appeared, the Siniavskii-Daniel trial had receded from public consciousness. See *A Survey of Iurii Trifonov's Work and an Analysis of the Moscow Novellas* (*Obzor tvorchestva i analiz moskovskikh povestei Iuriia Trifonova*) (Ann Arbor, Mich.: Ardis, 1983), 71.

15. Patera (ibid., 43–68) observes that the alterations made by the censors in the 1971 edition (as compared with the 1968 and 1978 texts) significantly weaken the impact of those references. The arrest scene itself disappears, for instance, as do some comments on the difficulties of life.

16. Trifonov, "How Our Word Resonates" (*Kak slovo nashe otzovetsia*), *Novyi mir* (November 1981): 235.

17. Lev Anninskii, "Intellectuals and Others" (*Intelligenty i drugie*), in *Tridtsatye-semidesiatye* (Moscow: Sovremennik, 1977), 211.

18. S. Eremina and V. Piskunov, "Time and Place in the Prose of Iurii Trifonov" (*Vremia i mesto prozy Iu. Trifonova*), *Voprosy literatury* (May 1982): 60–61.

19. Anninskii, "Intellectuals and Others," 211.

20. In his obituary for a close friend, the translator and essayist Lev Ginzburg, Trifonov praised his "everyday courage" as "courage of the highest sort: the courage of everyday, patient, stubborn." "In Memory of Lev Ginzburg," *Literaturnaia gazeta*, 1 October 1980, 15. Patera (*Survey of Iurii Trifonov's Work*, 193–94) believes that Ginzburg was the model for Gennadii Sergeevich.

21. "The late Stalinist epoch, nourished on suspicion toward any kind of dissident thought and 'disagreement,' was hardly an appropriate time for an enthusiasm of that nature. More—the study of 'disagreement' could, at that time, itself be easily taken for dissident thought." Patera, *Survey of Iurii Trifonov's Work*, 210.

22. See François de Liencourt, "The Repertoire of the Fifties," in *Literature and Revolution in Soviet Russia 1917–62*, 153–60.

23. G. Brovman, "The Measure of the Small World" (*Izmereniia malen'kogo mira*), *Literaturnaia gazeta*, 8 March 1972, 5. Republished in *Trud, geroi, literatura: ocherki i razmyshleniia o russkoi sovetskoi khudozhestvennoi proze* (Moscow, 1978): 225–36.

24. L. Libedinskaia, "Illusion and Reality" (*Iliuzii i real'nost'*), *Literaturnaia gazeta* 14 (1973): 6; V. Smirnova, "Private Life . . ." (*Lichnaia zhizn'* . . .), *Literaturnaia rossiia* 16 (1973): 10, 13; Iu. Idashkin, "Unsupported Variant" (*Nesostoiavshiisia variant*), *Oktiabr'* (August 1973): 203.

25. Anninskii, "Intellectuals and Others," 226.

26. "Romance with History: A Chat with Iu. Trifonov" (*Roman s istoriei: Beseda s Iu. Trifonovym*), *Voprosy literatury* (May 1982): 70. This is a translation and slight abridgment of the original, which appeared as "Gespräche

mit Juri Trifonov," *Weimarer Beiträge* 8 (1981): 142–48. Ralf Schröder, the journalist who interviewed Trifonov, describes the meeting in "My Year Hasn't Come Yet" (*Moi god eshche ne nastupil*), *Literaturnoe obozrenie* (August 1987): 96–98.

27. A. O., "Dichterische Deutung der Geschichte," *Neue Zürcher Zeitung*, 12–13 July 1975.

28. Vladimir Solov'ev, "About Love, and Not Only about Love" (*O liubvi, i ne tol'ko o liubvi*), *Literaturnoe obozrenie* (February 1976): 38.

29. Vladimir Dudintsev, "Is It Worth Dying before One's Time?" (*Stoit li umirat' ran'she vremeni*), *Literaturnoe obozrenie* (April 1976): 55. See also N. N. Shneidman, "Iurii Trifonov and the Ethics of Contemporary Soviet City Life," *Canadian Slavonic Papers* 19.3 (1977): 340–41.

30. Anninskii overlooks this closeness, exaggerating in his comment that "there is no contact, only ... lack of understanding" ("Cleansing by Means of the Past" [*Ochishchenie proshlym*], *Don* [February 1977]: 159).

31. I. Sozonova refutes Dudintsev's irascible article and offers a sympathetic reading of Olga in "Inside the Circle" (*Vnutri kruga*), *Literaturnoe obozrenie* (May 1976): 53–55.

32. Anatolii Bocharov, "Time of Crystallization" (*Vremia kristallizatsii*), *Voprosy literatury* (March 1976): 45–46.

33. V. Pertsovskii, "Authorial Position in Literature and Criticism" (*Avtorskaia pozitsiia v literature i kritike*), *Voprosy literatury* (July 1981): 99.

34. Sozonova, "Inside the Circle," 53.

II Young Men

1. Igor Dedkov, "Iurii Trifonov's Verticals" (*Vertikali Iuriia Trifonova*), *Novyi mir* (August 1985): 231.

2. The titles of some of the most popular novels of the 1970s are suggestive: Valentin Rasputin's *Farewell to Matera* (1976) and *Live and Remember* (1975); Vasilii Belov's *Eves* (1976).

3. Dmitrii Likhachev, "In the Service of Memory" (*Sluzhenie pamiati*), *Nash sovremennik* (March 1983): 171.

4. Cited in V. S. Sinenko, "The Possibilities of Artistic Synthesis" (*Vozmozhnosti khudozhestvennogo sinteza*), in *Zhanrovo-stilevye poiski sovetskoi literatury 70-kh godov*, ed. E. A. Nikulina (Leningrad: Izd. Leningradskogo universiteta, 1981), 50.

5. Ivanova, *The Prose of Iurii Trifonov*, 228. In the context of analyzing memory as the artistic organizing principle of *House on the Embankment*, she notes its similar function in Fedor Abramov's family saga, *The Priaslins*,

Belov's *Eves*, some short works by Kataev, and Aitmatov's *The Day Lasts Longer than the Century.*

6. Haney, "The Revival of Interest in the Russian Past."

7. Arkadii El'iashevich elliptically comments that Smolianov's professional decline coincides with the end "of that epoch in which the basic action of the novel is set" (i.e., Stalin's death in 1953). *Horizontals and Verticals (Gorizontali i vertikali)* (Leningrad: Sovetskii pisatel', 1984), 305.

8. Trifonov, "The Enigma and Clairvoyance of Dostoevskii" (*Zagadka i providenie Dostoevskogo*), *Novyi mir* (November 1981): 241–42. Reprinted as "Nechaev, Verkhovenskii i drugie . . . ," in *Kak slovo nashe otzovetsia* (Moscow: Sovremennaia rossiia, 1985), 38–52.

9. Trifonov, "Romance with History," 67.

10. Trifonov also gave Sergei many autobiographical experiences. Both character and author learned of Beria's arrest when they were on vacation at the beach. Sergei's father-in-law, Georgii Maksimovich, strongly resembles Trifonov's first wife's father, just as the room Sergei's in-laws live in resembles the room of Trifonov's in-laws.

11. Patera, *Survey of Iurii Trifonov's Work*, 231. It is she who points out that the years Sergei works on are the years of Bolshevik conflicts with the Mensheviks and the split in 1903; Trifonov doesn't mention them.

12. Ivanova, *The Prose of Iurii Trifonov*, 101.

13. Alexander Herzen, "Letter on the Freedom of the Will," cited by Isaiah Berlin, *Russian Thinkers* (New York: Penguin, 1978), 95.

14. "Trifonov endows Sergei with his own personal views on the moral design of history as science, his own intimate motives of regarding it. . . . Like Trifonov, Sergei seeks in history truthful self-awareness" (Pertsovskii, "Authorial Position in Literature and Criticism," 98).

15. Cited in Berlin, *Russian Thinkers*, 83–86, *passim.*

16. Ibid., 102.

17. Trifonov characterizes as "simple" those people who submit to such control (*liudi prostye, nevysokogo intellekta*), while "thinking" people (*mysliashchie*) oppose it (*AL* 273). Bocharov rightly dismisses this division as silly and contradicted elsewhere in Trifonov's work. Many "thinking" characters submit to manipulative, strong-willed people—Dmitriev to Lena in *The Exchange*, Grisha to his mother-in-law in *Long Goodbye*, Sergei to Olga. Bocharov, "Time of Crystallization," 46.

18. Ivanova, *The Prose of Iurii Trifonov*, 188–89.

19. Trifonov, "Romance with History," 67.

20. Igor Demidov, "The Past" (*Minuvshee*), *Teatr* (July 1981): 100–101.

21. Herzen, from "To an Old Comrade," cited in Berlin, *Russian Thinkers*, 101.

22. Sigrid McLaughlin, "Jurij Trifonov's *House on the Embankment*: Narration and Meaning," *Slavic and East European Journal* 26.4 (1982): 424.

23. When Iurii Liubimov was rehearsing the Taganka production of *House on the Embankment*, he prepared actors for the scene of the meeting with the following directions: "What cosmopolitanism is you must not explain. In the few minutes you're given you couldn't explain it anyway. Nor in hours, for that matter. But that's not our job anyway. You hold forth at the meeting, make speeches, throw around slogans, pin labels: 'We must strike!' 'Finish them off!' 'Tear it out by the roots!' 'Wipe it off the face of the earth!' 'Wrecker!' 'Spy!' 'Passportless!' 'Rootless!'—that's your entire vocabulary" (*udarit', pokonchit', iskorenit', smesti s litsa zemli, vreditel', agent, bespasportnyi, bezrodnyi*). Cited by Gershkovich, *Theater on the Taganka*, 22.

24. Trifonov, "Short Stay in a Torture Chamber" (*Nedolgoe prebyvanie v kamere pytok*), *Znamia* (December 1986): 123. The historian Iurii Feofanov, in a *glasnost'*-era article on the reclamation of Soviet history ("Return to the Truth," *Izvestiia*, 14 June 1988, 3), wrote much the same thing about what happened in 1936: "Rallies of workers, collective farmers, scientists, and cultural figures adopted resolutions, as did party *aktivs* and general meetings; certain of the country's most prominent citizens signed individual and collective letters expressing their devotion to Comrade Stalin. There was still no evidence against the accused, no verdict; yet the 'masses' were already aflame with malign enthusiasm. Society had turned into a mob. How sincere were all these resolutions calling for the defendants to be destroyed? I don't know, I can't confirm anything. But isn't a mob sincere in its savage impulses?"

25. Ivanova, *The Prose of Iurii Trifonov*, 224.

26. Bocharov, "Branches of One Trunk" (*Vetvi odnogo stvola*), in *Perspektiva o Sovetskoi literature zrelogo sotsializma*, ed. V. P. Balashov, E. N. Koniukhova, and A. A. Mikhailov (Moscow: Sovetskii pisatel', 1983), 368–70.

27. Primo Levi, *The Drowned and the Saved*, trans. Raymond Rosenthal (New York: Summit, 1988), 27–28.

28. V. S. Naipaul, *Bend in the River* (New York: Knopf, 1979), 141.

III Old Men

1. Valerii Golovskoi, "The Moral Lessons of Trifonov's Prose" (*Nravstvennye uroki Trifonovskoi prozy*), *Russian Language Journal* 37.128 (1983): 153–54.

2. The character of Migulin is based mainly on Filip Kuzmich Mironov, the Cossack military leader whom Trifonov first described in *The Campfire's Glow*. After forty-five years of silence Mironov's name was resurrected in an entry in the *Soviet Historical Encyclopedia* in 1966. For a factual

account of Mironov's career, including some of the documents Trifonov cites in *The Old Man*, see Roi Medvedev and Sergei Starikov, *Philip Mironov and the Russian Civil War* (New York: Knopf, 1978).

3. Alexander Yanov, *The New Russian Right* (Berkeley: Institute of International Studies, 1978), 7–9.

4. Ivanova puts the debate in the context of modern Soviet historiography, citing the work of S. B. Veselovskii and others. "A major Trifonov theme," she writes, "is developed in the argument about Ivan: can a man's actions be justified by the times? That is—can one hide behind the times, and then, when they have passed, fail to acknowledge them [*s nimi 'ne zdorovat'sia'*]" (*The Prose of Iurii Trifonov*, 238–40).

5. Jay Bergman, "The Perils of Historical Analogy: Leon Trotsky on the French Revolution," *Journal of the History of Ideas* 48.1 (1987): 73. For a discussion of the penetration of the myth of the French Revolution into the Russian revolutionary movement, see James Billington, *Fire in the Minds of Men: Origins of the Revolutionary Faith* (New York: Basic Books, 1983).

6. Herman Ermolaev interprets the argument about Ivan the Terrible in the context of the Civil War. The mass terror of the Civil War does not stem from any predisposition toward tyranny inherent in the character of the Russian people, which Trifonov represents metonymically in the figure of Ivan the Terrible. Rather, the terror stems from revolutionary ideology, as it did in the French Revolution. This explains the many parallels Trifonov establishes between Bolshevik and French terror. Ermolaev seems to turn Trifonov into an anti-Bolshevik, which he certainly was not. See "Past and Present in Iurii Trifonov's *The Old Man*" (*Proshloe i nastoiashchee v 'Starike' Iuriia Trifonova*), *Russian Language Journal* 37.128 (1983): 133.

7. Mikhail Sinel'nikov, "Get to Know the Man, Get to Know the Time" (*Poznat' cheloveka, poznat' vremia*), *Voprosy literatury* (September 1979): 45.

8. Helen Vendler, *The Odes of John Keats* (Cambridge and London: Harvard University Press, 1983), 132–33.

9. Abbott Gleason, *Young Russia* (New York: Viking, 1980), 338.

10. Vera Zasulich's description of Nechaev is strikingly apt: "[He] was not a product of our intelligentsia milieu. He was alien to it. It was not opinions, derived from contact with this milieu, which underlay his revolutionary energy, but burning hatred, and not only against the government, not only against institutions, not only against the exploiters of the people, but against all of *obshchestvo* [society], all educated strata, all these gentlefolk, rich and poor, conservative, liberal and radical." Cited in Gleason, *Young Russia*, 341.

11. Ivanova, *The Prose of Iurii Trifonov*, 252.

12. David Malouf, "House of the Dead," *New York Review of Books*, 12

March 1987, 8. Malouf is reviewing Robert Hughes's history of Australia, *The Fatal Shore*.

13. John Lewis Gaddis, "A Time of Confrontation and Confusion," *The Times Literary Supplement*, 8 May 1987, 479.

14. Bocharov, at pains to distinguish between Letunov's own evaluation of his behavior and Trifonov's, condemns Letunov for writing the article only when it became permissible. See "The Passion of the Struggle and Plaything Passions" (*Strast' bor'by i igrushechnye strasti*), *Literaturnoe obozrenie* (October 1978): 66. But before it "became permissible" it simply was *not* possible; at least Letunov took advantage of the new climate to write the piece.

15. Dedkov, "Iurii Trifonov's Verticals," 226–27.

16. Ivanova, *The Prose of Iurii Trifonov*, 254, 247.

17. Herzen, from "To an Old Comrade," cited in Berlin, *Russian Thinkers*, 101.

18. N. N. Shneidman comments, "The reminiscences of Letunov and his analysis of past events could lead the reader to conclusions which are very much in the spirit of Leo Tolstoi's interpretation of history. Man is a blind tool of circumstances. He participates in historical events, deluding himself that he is in possession of the truth, while in reality he is only emotionally attached to a cause without being able to make a rational decision about the real course of events." This, however, minimizes the distinction between the author and his protagonist. See *Soviet Literature in the 1970s* (Toronto: University of Toronto Press, n.d.), 99.

19. The version in *The Old Man* also suggests that the decossackization orders were the responsibility of the Don Revolutionary Committee rather than of the leadership in Moscow. "[Trifonov does not say] that the directive came from the very top of the Bolshevik government, was passed by the Organization Bureau of the Central Committee and signed by its chairman Iakov Sverdlov.... The omission of this fact automatically places all responsibility for the terror on the Bolshevik powers in the Don region, in the first place on the Don Revolutionary Committee" (Ermolaev, "Past and Present in Iurii Trifonov's *The Old Man*," 139).

20. Sinenko, "The Possibilities of Artistic Synthesis," 53–54.

21. Ermolaev, "Past and Present in Iurii Trifonov's *The Old Man*," 140.

22. In "Brief Stay in a Torture Chamber" Trifonov describes the guest book he read at a *pension* near Innsbruck. Its inscriptions dating from the war years hardly mention the war: the *pension*'s visitors were trying to forget it, at least for the duration of their stay. Their failure to mention the war does not make them malevolent liars, but it does make them unreliable and the document they left behind incomplete.

23. Milan Kundera includes a similar scene in his novel *The Farewell*

Party: a patrol goes around the town spying out dogs and impounding them. The dogcatchers are spiteful old men who have outlived all other means of exerting control; in a novel about victims and oppressors, they stand for—and with—the latter. The metaphor is effective in both books; no one likes dogcatchers.

24. Malouf, "House of the Dead," 8.

IV Pressures

1. Grigorii Svirskii is particularly harsh, commenting that with all the seeming independence of this "in-between" literature, its authors (Trifonov, Belov, Astaf'ev, Shukshin, and others) are part of a fundamentally lie-ridden political system. See *At the Execution Site: The Literature of Moral Opposition 1946–1976* (*Na lobnom meste: literatura nravstvennogo soprotivleniia*) (London: Overseas Publishing, 1979), 581–82. Other émigrés are more respectful, but essentially they agree. See, for instance, K. Shenfel'd, "Iurii Trifonov—Writer of Partial Truth" (*Iurii Trifonov—pisatel' chastichnoi pravdy*), *Grani* 121 (1981): 112–18; and Igor Efimov, "Writer among the Historians" (*Pisatel', raskonvoirovannyi v istoriki*), *Vremia i my* 71 (1983): 139–53.

2. See *Index on Censorship* 4 (August 1980) for several articles detailing the kinds and degree of censorship imposed in different disciplines in the Soviet Union in the 1960s and 1970s.

3. "There, behind the little window, there was something that didn't have a face but that was all-powerful and all-knowing: it alone could calm our fears. But it never did calm them." See Patera, *Survey of Iurii Trifonov's Work*, 148–50.

4. Peter Osnos, "Coping with the System," *The Guardian*, 11 June 1976.

5. Robert Toth, "New Novel Exalting Passivity Stirs a Controversy in Russia," *International Herald Tribune*, 25 May 1976 (reprinted from *Los Angeles Times*, 24 May 1976).

6. Ibid.

7. Sergei Iurenen, "*Druzhba narodov* Remains True to Yurii Trifonov's Memory," *Radio Liberty Research Report* 244 (30 July 1985) (translation of RS 85/85).

8. Olga Trifonova, personal interview, October 1986.

9. The 1978 two-volume collection of selected works, which contains every major work *except House on the Embankment*, was published in a print run of 100,000; the 1980 single volume containing *The Old Man* and *Another Life* came out in 200,000 copies.

10. Olga Trifonova, personal interview, October 1986.

11. The cuts and alterations in *The Old Man* were insignificant. See Golovskoi, "The Moral Lessons of Trifonov's Prose," 160–61.

12. Trifonov, "Notes of a Neighbor." The omitted portions were published as "Recalling Tvardovskii" (*Vspominaia Tvardovskogo*) in *Ogonek* 44 (1986).

13. Many émigrés have acknowledged this professional reality. See, for instance, Gladilin, *The Making and Unmaking of a Soviet Writer*, and Sergei Dovlatov's seriocomic *The Compromise* (New York: Knopf, 1983).

V   Narration

1. N. A. Kozhevnikova, "On the Correlation of Authorial Speech and Character's Speech" (*O sootnoshenii rechi avtora i personazha*), in *Iazykovye protsessy sovremennoi russkoi khudozhestvennoi literatury. Proza*, ed. A. I. Gorshkov and A. D. Grigor'eva (Moscow: Nauka, 1977), 21. In her analysis of trends in narrative voice in Soviet prose of the 1950s through 1970s, Kozhevnikova notes a general move away from the explicitly judgmental authorial point of view of earlier fiction.

2. Elsbeth Wolffheim, "Muss man sich der Tränen von einst erinnern?" *Neue Zürcher Zeitung*, 14 January 1983, 23.

3. See Katerina Clark, "Political History and Literary Chronotope," in *Literature and History: Theoretical Problems and Russian Case Studies*, ed. Gary Saul Morson (Stanford: Stanford University Press, 1986), 231–47, for an illuminating discussion of time-space concepts in Stalinist and post-Stalinist fiction.

4. Ivanova, *The Prose of Iurii Trifonov*, 265.

5. Bocharov, "Leaffall" (*Listopad*), *Literaturnoe obozrenie* (March 1981): 45.

6. Eremina and Piskunov, "Time and Place in the Prose of Iurii Trifonov," 45.

7. Bocharov, "Leaffall," 45.

8. Ivanova, *The Prose of Iurii Trifonov*, 265.

9. Elsa Morales attempted something comparable in *History: A Novel*, though she deliberately chose as her main characters people who—mistakenly—view themselves as being outside the influence of historical events. They are not. Often unaware of the meaning and direction of those events, they are nonetheless affected by them. Unlike Trifonov's highly educated and self-conscious characters, Morales's mother and children are simply "corks," always victims, never agents capable of changing history.

10. Ivanova, *The Prose of Iurii Trifonov*, 270–71.

11. M. Amusin, "Questions, Searches, Discoveries" (*Voprosy, poiski, obreteniia*), *Zvezda* (November 1982): 187.

12. See Ivanova, *The Prose of Iurii Trifonov*, 272–76; and Bocharov, "Leaffall."

13. D. Tevekelian, "Erase Accidental Features" (*Sotri sluchainye cherty*), *Novyi mir* (June 1982): 231.

14. For a brief summary of film treatment of the subject, see Anna Lawton, "Toward a New Openness," in *Post New Wave Cinema in the Soviet Union and Eastern Europe*, ed. Daniel J. Goulding (Bloomington: Indiana University Press, 1988), 31–34. See also N. Condee and V. Padunov, "Children at War: Films by Gubenko, Evtushenko and Bykov," *Framework* 30–31 (1986): 16–34.

15. See Vera Dunham, "Lyrics: The Pain of Discovery," in *Chronicle of a Revolution: A Western-Soviet Inquiry into Perestroika*, ed. A. Brumberg (New York: Pantheon, 1990), 139–42.

16. Wolffheim, "Muss man sich der Tränen von einst erinnern?" 23.

17. Likhachev, "In the Service of Memory," 171.

18. "I was often criticized for ... a 'dotted-line manner,' 'indistinctiveness' and worst of all, 'the absence of an explicit authorial stance,' ... [the last] a tag fraught with dire consequences for a writer" (I. Grekova, "Real Life in Real Terms," *Moscow News*, 21–28 June 1987, 11).

19. N. Klado, "The Procrustean Bed of *Byt*" (*Prokrustovo lozhe byta*), *Literaturnaia gazeta*, 12 May 1976, 4.

20. Iu. Surovtsev, "The Socialist Image of Life and Literature" (*Sotsialisticheskii obraz zhizni i literatura*), *Literaturnaia gazeta*, 9 June 1976, 2, 4. A number of critics defended Trifonov against the charge of indifference toward his heroes, including Arkadii El'iashevich, in *Horizontals and Verticals*, 277–83, *passim*.

21. For insights into the sources of acceptance of the affluence of the "new class," see Dunham, *In Stalin's Time*, 41–58.

22. Blurring authorial voice and characters' voices, Vadim Kozhinov claimed that Glebov's wish and ability to forget the past were Trifonov's as well. See "The Author's Problem and the Writer's Path" (*Problema avtora i put' pisatelia*), in *Kontekst 1977* (Moscow: Nauka, 1978), 23–47. Reprinted in *Stat'i o sovremennoi literature* (Moscow: Sovremennik, 1982), 212–34. When John Updike reviewed the English translation of *House on the Embankment*, he commented that Trifonov, intending to curse, "blessed" instead: "He portrays [Glebov] as timid, indecisive, and materialistic; yet the timidity and indecision are so empathetically limned, and the materialism ... such a basically humble attribute, that the reader, like Glebov's betrayed fiancée Sonya, loves him in spite of himself" ("Back in the U.S.S.R.," *The New Yorker*, 15 April 1985, 112). It is not clear how Updike reconciles

this with his view of the *I* (who certainly does not like Glebov) as a stand-in for the author.

23. Demidov, "The Past," 99–100.

24. McLaughlin, "Jurij Trifonov's *House on the Embankment*," 426.

25. Kozhevnikova, "On the Correlation of Authorial Speech and Character's Speech," 19–20.

26. McLaughlin, "Jurij Trifonov's *House on the Embankment*," 420.

27. Ibid., 420.

28. A. Mikhailov, "Who's Next?" (*Kto sleduiushchii*), *Oktiabr'* (December 1984): 189. The specific text he refers to is a story by Boris Roshchin in which two narrators and two narratives are interwoven.

29. Eremina and Piskunov, "Time and Place in the Prose of Iurii Trifonov," 54–55.

30. Bocharov, "Leaffall," 46. Trifonov's attempt to split himself is "connected with the desire to evaluate one's life, to see into the inner exploding heart of the contradiction, strip off its skin to reveal the pulsing, beating truth."

31. R. Luplow, "Narrative Style and Structure in *One Day in the Life of Ivan Denisovich*," *Russian Literature Triquarterly* 1 (1971): 401.

32. Hosking, *Beyond Socialist Realism*, 45.

33. Eremina and Piskunov trace the pattern of deaths throughout the book, in "Time and Place in the Prose of Iurii Trifonov," 47–49.

34. Ivanova, *The Prose of Iurii Trifonov*, 231.

35. See Galina Belaia, *The Aesthetic World of Contemporary Prose* (*Khudozhestvennyi mir sovremennoi prozy*) (Moscow: Nauka, 1983), 166–67.

36. Ivanova, *The Prose of Iurii Trifonov*, 280–82. She discusses the general trend toward explicit authorial presence—and a lyric voice close to the author's—in "Free Breathing" (*Vol'noe dykhanie*), *Voprosy literatury* (March 1983) (reprinted in *Tochka zreniia* [Moscow: Sovetskii pisatel', 1988], 6–40).

37. Anatolii Bocharov, personal interview, November 1986.

38. A. Mikhailov, "The Expanse of the Story" (*Prostranstvo rasskaza*), *Oktiabr'* (January 1986): 178–79.

VI *Byt*

1. Trifonov, "Grey Sky, Masts and a Chestnut Horse" (*Seroe nebo, machty i ryzhaia loshad'*), *Novyi mir* (July 1981): 85.

2. M. M. Bakhtin, "Forms of Time and of the Chronotope in the Novel," in *The Dialogic Imagination*, trans. Caryl Emerson and Michael Holquist (Austin: University of Texas Press, 1981), 84.

3. Clark, "Political History and Literary Chronotope," 239.

4. Mikhailov, "Who's Next?" 190.

5. See Maguire, *Red Virgin Soil*, 189–90, for a discussion of the polemics surrounding the concept of *byt* in the early Soviet period.

6. Hosking, *Beyond Socialist Realism*, 40.

7. Grekova, "Real Life in Real Terms."

8. See, for instance, Iu. Andreev, "In the Closed World" (*V zamknutom mire*), *Literaturnaia gazeta*, 3 March 1971, 5; V. I. Ozerov, "Literary-Artistic Criticism and the Contemporary Period" (*Literaturno-khudozhestvennaia kritika i sovremennost'*), *Voprosy literatury* (April 1972): 24–25; V. Sokolov, "The Splintering of the Everyday" (*Rasshcheplenie obydennosti*), *Voprosy literatury* (February 1972): 31–45; M. Sinel'nikov, "The Ordeal of Daily Life" (*Ispytanie povsednevnost'iu*), *Voprosy literatury* (February 1972): 46–62; V. Gogolev, "Problems of *Byt* and Problems of People" (*Problemy byta i problemy liudei*), in *Tverskoi bul'var* 25.14 (1974): 143–55.

9. Trifonov, "How Our Word Resonates," 235. Reprinted in *Kak slovo nashe otzovetsia*, 310. In the notes to the latter version (379, n. 1) Anninskii reports that Trifonov asked him to "pitch him a ball" about *byt*; he wanted the opportunity to answer his critics and had prepared a response in writing.

10. Anninskii, "Cleaving the Root: On Iurii Trifonov's Publicistic Writing" (*Rassechenie kornia: o publitsistike Iuriia Trifonova*), preface to *Kak slovo nashe otzovetsia*, 14.

11. Bocharov, "Branches from One Trunk," 363–64.

12. Bocharov, "In the Interests of Depth: Notes on Artistic Truth" (*V pol'zu glubiny: zametki o khudozhestvennoi pravde*), *Novyi mir* (March 1984): 225–26.

13. Eremina and Piskunov, "Time and Place in the Prose of Iurii Trifonov," 62.

14. See Amusin, "Questions, Searches, Discoveries," 182–91, for a discussion of how the "small world" of private life and the "large world" of history penetrate and depend on each other in Trifonov's work.

15. Wolffheim, "Muss man sich der Tränen von einst erinnern?" 23.

16. The Byzantine complexities of Soviet housing and the paucity of apartments explain Lena's dream of finding someone willing to exchange one two-room flat for two one-room flats in different locations. A variety of tenants might be interested: a divorcing couple, for instance, who want to live separately but would otherwise have to wait years for individual housing, or a family whose grown child has married and needs a place of his or her own. It should be kept in mind that when Soviets count rooms in a flat (as in a two-room apartment), they routinely exclude kitchen and bathroom.

17. Eremina and Piskunov, "Time and Place in the Prose of Iurii Trifonov," 58–59.

18. Ibid., 62.

19. Ivanova, *The Prose of Iurii Trifonov*, 263.

20. Ibid., 263.

21. For a detailed description of the house by a former resident, see the excerpts from Lidiia Shatunovskaia's memoirs: "House on the Embankment" (*Dom na naberezhnoi*), *Kontinent* 23 (1980): 235–54, and "Day of Reckoning" (*Chas rasplaty*), *Kontinent* 27 (1981): 325–41.

22. Anne G. Hughes, reply to a letter in *Canadian Slavonic Papers* 23.2 (1981), 208. In her view Levka the gatekeeper also personifies "certain aspects of the Stalin era that, although supposedly relegated to the underworld, long to return to the light and are biding their time."

23. The house still stands, though the kind of tenements in which Glebov lived as a child disappeared long ago. Wall plaques commemorate some of its more famous inhabitants, such as Marshall Tukhachevskii. Though run-down and shabby, its apartments are still unusual for their high ceilings, spacious dimensions, and spectacular views of the Moscow River.

24. Thus designer David Borovskii's set for the Taganka production was exceptionally appropriate, with its glass walls of the house separating past and present.

25. *The Disappearance* served Trifonov as a kind of notebook for other works. *House on the Embankment* is the published work closest to it, but *Time and Place* incorporates certain scenes and characters, such as the family of three generations of women.

26. Natalia Gross speculated that the stories were approved for publication because they sharply condemn emigration. "This element balances the criticism of Soviet society. . . . The writer adheres to the current literary policy in that he supports the ideas of patriotism and national unity—in other words, the might and monolithic nature of the Soviet totalitarian state" ("Homage to Yurii Trifonov," *Radio Liberty Research Report* 426 [27 October 1981], translation of RS 176/81). Her political approach ignores Trifonov's elegiac tone, which radically undercuts—indeed contradicts—"current literary policy."

27. Ivanova, *The Prose of Iurii Trifonov*, 285.

28. Trifonov recounted the episode more than once. In "A Neighbor's Notes" he identifies the editor who rejected his stories as Zaks, and (530) quotes Zaks' laconic dismissal: "Some sort of universal themes."

29. Bocharov, "Branches of One Trunk," 369–70.

VII   The Alchemy of Art

1. Anthony Austin, "Yuri Trifonov, Noted Soviet Author, Dies at Age 55," *New York Times*, 29 March 1981.

2. V. Kardin, "The Times Do Not Choose . . ." (*Vremena ne vybiraiut . . .*), *Novyi mir* (July 1987): 256.

3. Anatolii Rybakov, *Children of the Arbat* (*Deti Arbata*), *Druzhba narodov* (June 1987): 151. The lines conclude an authorial epilogue omitted from the English text.

4. Tevekelian, "Erase Accidental Features," 232.

5. This interpretation was offered by Olga Trifonova (personal interview, November 1986).

6. Mikhailov, "From the First Person" (*Ot pervogo litsa*), *Oktiabr'* (January 1983): 186.

7. Bulat Okudzhava describes what *he*, about the same age as Sasha, expected from his mother's return in 1947, and how the reality differed from his anticipation. See "Girl of My Dreams" (*Devushka moei mechty*), *Druzhba narodov* (October 1986).

8. It is an evasion common to Trifonov's heroes. Shura's illness in *The Old Man* allows him to escape from the Slaboserdov murder he is helpless to prevent; Gennadii Sergeevich, in *Taking Stock*, exploits his heart condition whenever he cannot deal with circumstances.

9. This was a favorite procedure for Soviet writers during Stalin's years and subsequently. See Clark, *The Soviet Novel*, 147–52. Kathleen Parthé points out how often such "collecting" in later years lacked context and meaning, even among writers who themselves came from villages. See "Images of Rural Transformation in Russian Village Prose," *Studies in Comparative Communism* 23.2 (Summer 1990): 161–76.

10. Sasha's mistress, for instance, is mirrored in Nikiforov's wife, Georgina. Both women simultaneously inspire and destroy their men's literary gifts. Georgina, mirroring Kiianov's wife, is held responsible for his moral compromises.

11. Most, but not all, of these kinds of attacks stopped with Trifonov's death. In M. Amusin's generally favorable article, for instance, Trifonov is faulted for ignoring the "social resonance" of his characters' moral choices. See "Questions, Searches, Discoveries," 184–85.

12. Ivanova, *The Prose of Iurii Trifonov*, 267–68.

13. Belaia points out how often Trifonov used impersonal verbs (*konchilos'*, *dlilos'*, *zhilos'*) to suggest the irrational reasons for the dwindling of human relationships (*The Aesthetic World of Contemporary Prose*, 173).

14. Galina Belaia, *Literature in the Mirror of Criticism* (*Literature v zerkale*

kritiki) (Moscow: Sovetskii pisatel', 1986), 196. In Belaia's view Trifonov almost always undercuts his heroes' and heroines' simplistic notions of changing fate.

15. Mikhailov, "From the First Person," 186.

16. Given the many parallels, it is impossible to credit as serious Vadim Kozhinov's hypothesis that Trifonov might have rewritten *Students* "completely unconsciously" ("The Author's Problem and the Writer's Path," 220).

17. Kozhinov faults Trifonov precisely for failing explicitly to condemn Glebov. He evidently would like a literal rejection of the positive hero Trifonov created (and admired) in *Students*; without such rejection, he asserts, Trifonov fails to exculpate himself.

18. Ivanova, *The Prose of Iurii Trifonov*, 234.

19. Pertsovskii, "Authorial Position in Literature and Criticism," 102–3.

20. Bocharov, "Leaffall," 47.

Conclusion

1. Helena Goscilo, "Alternative Prose and *Glasnost* Literature," in *Five Years that Shook the World: Gorbachev's Revolution*, ed. H. Balzer (Boulder, Colo.: Westview Press, 1991). She includes among those shortcomings "wooden dialogue, characters that fail to come alive, interminable harangues, shaky transitions and faltering command of viewpoint."

2. Recent Soviet writing on the rehabilitation of Bukharin and other Old Bolsheviks explicitly connects the moral relativity of their behavior with the Stalinist repressions. See, for instance, Evgenii Ambartsumov, "A Venomous Fog Lifts," *Moscow News*, 19 June 1988.

3. Zolotusskii, "The Ennobling Word," 15–16. See also Toporov, "Phenomenon of Disappearance," 22.

4. Goscilo, "Alternative Prose and *Glasnost* Literature."

Selected Bibliography

Works by Iurii Trifonov
In Russian

Izbrannye proizvedeniia v dvukh tomakh. 2 vols. Moscow: Khudozhestvennaia literatura, 1978. Volume 1 contains twenty-six stories and *Neterpenie;* volume 2 contains *Obmen, Predvaritel'nye itogi, Dolgoe proshchanie, Drugaia zhizn',* stories, and articles.

Starik/Drugaia zhizn'. Moscow: Sovetskii pisatel', 1980.

Kak slovo nashe otzovetsia. . . . Moscow: Sovetskaia rossiia, 1985. Articles and interviews.

Vechnye temy. Moscow: Sovetskii pisatel', 1985. Contains *Starik, Vremia i mesto, Drugaia zhizn',* and *Oprokinutyi dom.*

Sobranie sochinenii v chetyrekh tomakh. 4 vols. Moscow: Khudozhestvennaia literatura, 1987. Volume 1 contains *Studenty* and *Utolenie zhazhdy;* volume 2 contains *Dolgoe proshchanie, Dom na naberezhnoi, Drugaia zhizn', Obmen,* and *Predvaritel'nye itogi;* volume 3 contains *Neterpenie* and *Starik;* volume 4 contains *Otblesk kostra, Vremia i mesto,* a variety of articles, and eleven stories, including the stories comprising *Oprokinutyi dom.*

Ischeznovenie. Moscow: Moskovskii rabochii, 1988. Contains *Ischeznovenie, Otblesk kostra,* and *Starik.*

Vremia i mesto. Moscow: Izvestiia, 1988. Contains *Dom na naberezhnoi, Ischeznovenie* and *Vremia i mesto.*

In English

Students. Moscow: Foreign Languages Publishing House, 1953.
"Thirst aquenched." *Soviet Literature* (January 1964).

161

The Impatient Ones. Moscow: Progress Publishing House, 1978.
The Long Goodbye. Ann Arbor, Mich.: Ardis, 1979. Contains *The Exchange, Taking Stock,* and *The Long Goodbye.*
Another Life/The House on the Embankment. New York: Simon and Schuster, 1983.
The Old Man. New York: Simon and Schuster, 1984.

Secondary Sources

A. O. "Dichterische Deutung der Geschichte." *Neue Zürcher Zeitung,* 12–13 July 1975.
Amlinskii, Vladimir. "O dniakh edinstvennykh." *Literaturnoe obozrenie* (January 1982): 42–45.
Amusin, M. "Voprosy, poiski, obreteniia." *Zvezda* (November 1982): 182–91.
Anninskii, Lev. "Intelligenty i prochie." *Tridtsatye-semidesiatye.* Moscow: Sovremennik, 1977, 197–227.
———. "Neokonchatel'nye itogi: o trekh povestiakh Iuriia Trifonova." *Don* (May 1972): 183–92.
———. "Ochishchenie proshlym." *Don* (February 1977): 157–60.
———. "Rassechenie kornia: o publitsistike Iuriia Trifonova." Preface to *Kak slovo nashe otzovetsia,* ed. A. P. Shitov, 3–20. Moscow: Sovremennaia rossiia, 1985.
Austin, Anthony. "An Advance for Soviet Candor." *New York Times,* 8 May 1980.
———. "Yuri Trifonov, Noted Soviet Author, Dies at Age 55." *New York Times,* 29 March 1981.
Beerman, Rene. "Auf der Suche nach einem Sinn des Lebens: Notizen über die sowjetrussische Gegenswartsliteratur." *Osteuropa* 27.9 (1977): 753–66.
Belaia, Galina. "Nravstvennyi mir khudozhestvennogo proizvedeniia." *Voprosy literatury* (April 1983): 19–52. (Reprinted in *Khudozhestvennyi mir sovremennoi prozy.* Moscow: Nauka, 1983, 151–84.)
———. "O 'vnutrennei' i 'vneshnei' teme." *Literatura v zerkale kritiki.* Moscow: Sovetskii pisatel', 1986, 158–201.
———. "Pozdniaia zarnitsa na kraiu zhizni . . ." *Puteshestvie v poiskakh istiny.* Tbilisi: Merani, 1987, 157–83.
Bocharov, Anatolii. *Beskonechnost' poiska. Khudozhestvennye poiski sovremennoi sovetskoi prozy.* Moscow: Sovetskii pisatel', 1982, 102–16.
———. "Listopad." *Literaturnoe obozrenie* (March 1982): 45–48.
———. "Rozhdeno sovremennost'iu." *Novyi mir* (August 1981): 227–46.

———. "Strast' bor'by i igrushechnye strasti." *Literaturnoe obozrenie* (October 1978): 64–67.

———. "Vetvi odnogo stvola." In *Perspektiva o sovetskoi literature zrelogo sotsializma,* ed. V. P. Balashov, E. N. Koniukhova, and A. A. Mikhailov. Moscow: Sovetskii pisatel', 1983.

———. "Vremia kristallizatsii." *Voprosy literatury* (March 1976): 29–57.

Bourg, Charles Alain. "Le rôle du mystère dans le Vieil Homme de Jurij Trifonov." *Essais sur le discours sovietique* 3 (1983): 64–86.

Brown, Edward. "Trifonov: The Historian as Artist." In *Soviet Society and Culture: Essays in Honor of Vera S. Dunham,* ed. Terry L. Thompson and Richard Sheldon. Boulder, Colo.: Westview Press, 1988, 109–23.

Clark, Katerina. "The Mutability of the Canon: Socialist Realism and Chingiz Aitmatov's *I dol'she veka dlitsia den'." Slavic Review* 43.4 (1984): 573–87.

———. "Political History and Literary Chronotope: Some Soviet Case Studies." In *Literature and History: Theoretical Problems and Russian Case Studies,* ed. Gary Saul Morson. Stanford: Stanford University Press, 1986, 230–46.

———. *The Soviet Novel: History as Ritual.* Chicago: University of Chicago Press, 1981.

Dedkov, Igor. "Vertikali Iuriia Trifonova." *Novyi mir* (August 1985): 220–35.

De Maegd-Soëp, Carolina. *Trifonov and the Drama of the Russian Intelligentsia.* Gent: Russian Institute, 1990.

Demidov, A. "Minuvshee." *Teatr* (July 1981): 97–107.

Dudintsev, Vladimir. "Stoit li umirat' ran'she vremeni." *Literaturnoe obozrenie* (April 1976): 52–57.

———. "Velikii smysl—zhit'." *Literaturnoe obozrenie* (May 1976): 48–52.

Dumrath, F. *Die Funktion des Präsens im Roman "Starik" von Jurij V. Trifonov.* Hamburg: Busker, 1982.

Dunham, Vera. *In Stalin's Time: Middleclass Values in Soviet Fiction.* Cambridge: Cambridge University Press, 1976.

Durkin, Andrew R. "The Role of Čexovian Subtext." *Slavic and East European Journal* 28.1 (1984): 32–41.

Druzhnikov, Iurii. "Sud'ba Trifonova: dva puti za granitsu." *Vremia i my* 1 (1990): 247–78.

El'iashevich, Arkadii. "Chelovek v masshtabe vremeni." *Zvezda* (May 1982): 166–81.

———. "Gorod i gorozhane. O tvorchestve Iuriia Trifonova." *Gorizontali i vertikali.* Leningrad: Sovetskii pisatel', 1984, 255–366.

———. "Literatura semidesiatykh: monologi i dialogi." *Zvezda* (March

1979): 191–210. (Translated in *Soviet Studies in Literature* 15 (1978–79): 26–73.)

Eremina, S., and V. Piskunov. "Vremia i mesto prozy Iuriia Trifonova." *Voprosy literatúry* (May 1982): 34–64.

Ermolaev, German. "Proshloe i nastoiashchee v 'Starike' Iuriia Trifonova." *Russian Language Journal* 128 (1983): 131–45.

Garrard, John, and Carol Garrard. *Inside the Soviet Writers' Union.* New York: Free Press, 1990.

Gasiorowska, Xenia. "Two Decades of Love and Marriage in Soviet Fiction." *Russian Review* 1 (1975): 10–22.

Gelhard, Susanna. *Die Dramatisierung von Jurij Valentinovic Trifonovs Roman "Das Haus an der Moskva" am Moskauer Taganka-Theater.* Mainz: Liber, 1984.

Gibian, George. "The Urban Theme in Recent Soviet Prose: Notes toward a Typology." *Slavic Review* 37.1 (1978): 40–51.

Gillespie, David C. "Time, History, and the Individual in the Works of Yury Trifonov." *Modern Language Review* 83.2 (1988): 375–95.

Gladil'shchikov, Iurii. "Ne ischeznovenie. Pamiat' . . ." *Literaturnaia rossiia,* 27 March 1987.

Golovskoi, Valerii. "Nravstvennye uroki Trifonovskoi prozy." *Russian Language Journal* 128 (1983): 147–61.

Gross, Nataliya. "Homage to Yurii Trifonov." *Radio Liberty Research Report* 426/81 (translation of RS 176/81, 27 October 1981).

Gusev, Vladimir. "Prostranstvo slova." *Pamiat' i stil'.* Moscow: Sovetskii pisatel', 1981, 324–33.

Haussmann, Christiane. *Der Sowjetische Mensch in Der Krise.* Ph.D. diss., Tübingen University, 1983.

Hughes, Anne C. "*Bol'shoi mir* or *zamknutoi mirok*: Departure from Literary Convention in Iurii Trifonov's Recent Fiction." *Canadian Slavonic Papers* 22.4 (1980): 470–80.

Ivanova, Natalia. *Proza Iuriia Trifonova.* Moscow: Sovetskii pisatel', 1984.

————. "Vol'noe dykhanie." *Voprosy literatury* (March 1983): 179–214.

Jokostra, Peter. "Verschuttete Wahrheiten." *Die Welt,* 18 June 1977.

Kardin, V. "Vremena ne vybiraiut . . ." *Novyi mir* (July 1987): 236–57.

Kenez, Peter. "Trifonov's Russia." *The New Leader,* 10 September 1979.

Kling, O. Review of *Khudozhestvennyi mir sovremennoi prozy,* by Galina Belaia. *Voprosy literatury* (June 1984): 232–38.

Kozhevnikova, N. A. "O sootnoshenii rechi avtora i personazha." In *Iazykovye protsessy sovremennoi russkoi khudozhestvennoi literatury. Proza,* ed. A. I. Gorshkov and A. D. Grigor'eva, 7–98. Moscow: Nauka, 1977.

Kozhinov, Vadim. "Problema avtora i put' pisatelia: na materiale dvukh povestei Iuriia Trifonova." *Stat'i o sovremennoi literature*. Moscow: Sovremennik, 1982, 213–34.

Kuzicheva, A. "Iurii Trifonov: 'Obmen,' 'Dolgoe proshchanie,' 'Drugaia zhizn,' ego geroev i chitatelei." *Knizhnoe obozrenie*, 8 April 1988.

McLaughlin, Sigrid. "Iurii Trifonov's *Dom na naberezhnoi* and Dostoevskii's *Prestuplenie i nakazanie*." *Canadian Slavonic Papers* 25.2 (1983): 275–83.

————. "Jurij Trifonov's *House on the Embankment*: Narration and Meaning." *Slavic and East European Journal* 26.4 (1982): 419–33.

Malt'sev, Iurii. "Promezhutochnaia literatura i kriterii podlinnosti." *Kontinent* 25 (1980): 285–321.

Mikhailov, A. "Kto sleduiushchii?" *Oktiabr'* (December 1984): 186–92.

————. "Ot pervogo litsa." *Oktiabr'* (January 1983): 182–89.

————. "Prostranstvo rasskaza." *Oktiabr'* (January 1986): 179–89.

Natov, Nadine. "Daily Life and Individual Psychology in Soviet-Russian Prose of the 1970s." *Russian Review* 4 (1974): 357–71.

Oklianskii, Iurii. *Iurii Trifonov: Portret-vospominaniia*. Moscow: Sovetskaia rossiia, 1987.

————. "'Schastlivye neudachniki' Iuriia Trifonova." *Literaturnoe obozrenie* (November 1985): 103–12.

Osnos, Peter. "Coping with the System." *Guardian*, 11 June 1976.

Pankin, Boris. "Circle or Spiral?" In *Demanding Literature: Soviet Literature of the 1970s and early 1980s*, trans. Ruth English. Moscow: Raduga, 1984, 156–97.

Patera, Tatiana. *Obzor tvorchestva i analiz moskovskikh povestei Iuriia Trifonova*. Ann Arbor, Mich.: Ardis, 1983.

Pertsovskii, V. "'Avtorskaia pozitsiia' v literature i kritike." *Voprosy literatury* (July 1981): 66–106.

————. *Prodolzhenie poiska. Literaturno-kriticheskie stat'i raznykh let*. Novosibirsk: Zapadno-Sibirskoe knizhnoe izdatel'stvo, 1984.

Reissner, Eberhard. "Auf der Suche nach der verlorenen Wahrheit: Jurij Trifonows jüngster Roman *Der Alte*." *Osteuropa* 29.2 (1979): 99–109.

Schmid, W. "Thesen zur innovatorischen Poetik der russischen Gegenwartsprosa." *Wiener Slawistischer Almanach* 4 (1979): 55–93.

Shklovskii, Evgenii. "Fenomen zhizni." *Literaturnoe obozrenie* (April 1986): 66–69.

————. "Pafos—issledovanie." Review of *Prodolzhenie poiska*, by V. Pertsovskii. *Voprosy literatury* (November 1984): 226–32.

————. "Po verkhnomu sloiu: zametki o konflikte i geroe v zhurnal'noi proze." *Literaturnoe obozrenie* (July 1985): 27–33.

Shneidman, N. N. "Iurii Trifonov and the Ethics of Contemporary Soviet City Life." *Canadian Slavonic Papers* 19.3 (1977): 335–51.

————. "The New Dimensions of Time and Place in Iurii Trifonov's Prose of the 1980s." *Canadian Slavonic Papers* 27.2 (1985): 188–95.

————. *Soviet Literature in the 1970s: Artistic Diversity and Ideological Conformity.* Toronto: University of Toronto Press, n.d.

Sidorov, Evgenii. Review of *Beskonechnost' poiska,* by A. Bocharov. *Voprosy literatury* (April 1983): 222–26.

————. *Vremia, pisatel', stil': O sovetskoi proze nashikh dnei.* Moscow: Sovetskii pisatel', 1978.

Sinel'nikov, Mikhail. "Ispytanie povsednevnost'iu: nekotorye itogi." *Voprosy literatury* (February 1972): 46–62.

————. "Poznat' cheloveka, poznat' vremia . . . : O 'Starike' Iuriia Trifonova." *Voprosy literatury* (September 1979): 26–52.

Sinenko, V. S. "Vozmozhnosti khudozhestvennogo sinteza." In *Zhanrovostilevye poiski sovetskoi literatury 70-kh godov,* ed. E. A. Nikulina. Leningrad: Izd. Leningradskogo universiteta, 1981, 48–56.

Sokolov, V. "Rasshcheplenie obydennosti." *Voprosy literatury* (February 1972): 31–45.

Solov'ev, Vladimir. "O liubvi, i ne tol'ko o liubvi . . ." *Literaturnoe obozrenie* (February 1976): 38–40.

Sozonova, I. "Vnutri kruga." *Literaturnoe obozrenie* (May 1976): 53–55.

Szenfeld, Ignacy. "Yurii Trifonov's New Novel *Starik.*" *Radio Liberty Research Report* 183/78 (translation of RS 87/78, 23 August 1978).

Tevekelian, D. "Sotri sluchainye cherty." *Novyi mir* (June 1982): 216–34.

Toporov, Viktor. "Fenomen ischeznoveniia." *Literaturnoe obozrenie* (January 1988): 22–25.

Toth, Robert. "New Novel Exalting Passivity Stirs a Controversy in Russia." *International Herald Tribune,* 25 May 1976.

Updike, John. "Back in the U.S.S.R." *The New Yorker,* 15 April 1985, 110–26.

Velembovskaia, Irina. "Simpatii i antipatii Iuriia Trifonova." *Novyi mir* (September 1980): 255–58.

von Ssachno, Helen. "Denkmal fur einen Hingerichteten." *Süddeutsche Zeitung,* 31 May 1978.

Vozdvizhenskii, Viacheslav. "Prostor Trifonovskoi prozy." Review of *Proza Iuriia Trifonova,* by N. Ivanova. *Voprosy literatury* (January 1986): 245–53.

Whitney, Craig. "Russian Writer, Not a Dissident, Critic of Society." *New York Times,* 24 October 1977.

————. "USSR—The Legacy of Stalin." *New York Times,* 16 December 1979.

Wolffheim, Elsbeth. "Muss man sich der Tränen von einst erinnern?" *Neue Zürcher Zeitung,* 14 January 1983.

Zolotusskii, Igor. "Vozvyshaiushchee slovo." *Literaturnoe obozrenie* (July 1988): 7–18.

Index

About the Author

Josephine Woll is Associate Professor of Russian Literature at Howard University and received her Ph.D. from the University of North Carolina at Chapel Hill. She is the coauthor of *Soviet Dissident Literature: A Critical Guide,* and she writes often about Russian and Soviet cultural issues.

About the Author

Josephine Woll is Associate Professor of Russian Literature at Howard University and received her Ph.D. from the University of North Carolina at Chapel Hill. She is the coauthor of *Soviet Dissident Literature: A Critical Guide,* and she writes often about Russian and Soviet cultural issues.